708 RUN

ST

WITHDRAWN FROM LIBRARY STOCK

SOUTHAM

DUCATION

2731908

WITHDRAWN FROM LIBRARY STOCK

REFERENCE ONLY
DO NOT REMOVE
FROM THE LIBRARY

MUSEUMS & GALLERIES COMMISSION

The
Museum
Marketing
Handbook

LONDON: HMSO

© Crown copyright 1994
Applications for reproduction should be made to HMSO

ISBN 0 11 290517 X

British Library Cataloguing in Publication Data
A CIP catalogue record for this book is
available from the British Library

The Author

Sue Runyard was previously Head of Press & Information at the Victoria & Albert Museum and the Natural History Museum, and Press Officer to Lord Gowrie as Minister for the Arts, and Lord Young as Minister Without Portfolio. For the past six years she has been working with museums of all kinds throughout the United Kingdom as Marketing & Development Adviser to the Museums & Galleries Commission. She is a member of the Chartered Institute of Marketing.

Written for the Museums & Galleries Commission by Sue Runyard.
Photography by Robynne Limoges.

SOUTHAMPTON INSTITUTE OF HIGHER
EDUCATION LIBRARY
Bookseller: 21   Location:
Requisition No.:
Class No:
Acc. No.:   Date: 20-7-94

Front cover illustration:
National Waterways Museum, Gloucester, photo by Robynne Limoges.

Contents

Introduction   5

How to write a Marketing Strategy   7

A to Z of Museum Marketing Methods   17
   Advertising   17
   Budgets   24
   Corporate Identity   27
   Distribution   30
   Emergency Plans   32
   Fundraising   36
   Group Travel   37
   Helpful Publications   40
   Incentives   42
   Joint Schemes   44
   Know Your Market   45
   Literature   49
   Monitoring/Evaluation   54
   New Markets   57
   Opinion Forming   59
   Press Relations   61
   Quotability   65
   Research   65
   Strategic Planning   67
   Targeting   68
   Using Consultants   70
   Value for Money   72
   Writing Skills   73
   X Factor   74
   Yield   75
   Zap Lists   77

Case Studies   81
   A Short-Term Museum Marketing Consultancy   83
   Museums Alive!: Museums Marketing Together
      in Yorkshire & Humberside   91
   A Visitor Attendance Consultancy: Ruddington   101
   A Large Museum Marketing Plan:
      Manchester Museum of Science & Industry   111
   A Small Museum Marketing Plan:
      Regiments of Gloucester Museum   119
   Creating a Climate for Customer Care:
      Dr Patrick Greene   124

Devising Your Marketing Plan:
  Gerri Morris   *128*
  Appointing a Marketing Officer   *131*

Glossary   *134*

Acorn Classifications   *135*

Index   *139*

INTRODUCTION

A recognition of the importance of marketing came to museums just as the UK entered an economic recession. It is also true to say that other areas of work were also newly recognised as important – from proper environmental controls to access for people with disabilities. This made for some very difficult decisions on priorities, and still does.

What greatly assists the case for marketing is that, starting from a low baseline, it is virtually always effective. And, being effective, it assists the survival of the museum.

Previous publications have drawn attention to the need for better marketing in museums. The Museums & Galleries Commission, in successive reports, has said that museums need marketing officers. In the report *Local Authorities and Museums*, (1991), the MGC recommends museums to share marketing managers if they cannot employ one full-time; encourages collaboration in joint marketing schemes; and asks Area Museum Councils to consider the appointment of marketing advisers. Some progress has been made. The later MGC Report *Management Development and Marketing in Museums* (1992) shows that full-time marketing posts grew from 5 in 1988 to approaching 40 in 1992. Indications are that this trend will continue, although there is obviously some way to go.

The Office of Arts and Libraries *Report on the Development of Performance Indicators for the National Museums and Galleries* (1991) laid stress on the importance of market research in the improvement of quality of service and development of performance indicators. The Audit Commission's *The Road to Wigan Pier?*, also published in February 1991, advocates a marketing approach and says that 'promotion is essential'. Other reports have made similar points.

This book is aimed at the people in museums who no longer need persuading that marketing is useful, but want to know how to do it; how to plan for it; and what other people have achieved. Tyne and Wear Museums are a case in point. Under new directorship in 1991, they decided, despite conflicting demands on resources, to establish a professional marketing office. They have not regretted their decision. In 1992 their attendance figures doubled and they enjoy an increasingly high profile and a greater sense of identity. Tourist boards have been impressed by the performance of museums throughout the recession. Of all parts of the leisure/attractions industry, museums seem to be performing best in attracting more people, and better marketing is seen as a major factor. We know it works. At its best, it contributes to quality as much as quantity. The next steps are to introduce marketing where there is none, to improve it where it already exists, and to think of ever more creative ways to make it serve museums.

1.   Reflections in a museum.

HOW TO WRITE A MARKETING STRATEGY

A Sense Of Identity

To get from A to B you need to know a great deal about your starting point. Clarity of thought about objectives and processes is a vital asset, but there is no substitute for good information.

Often a museum or gallery will start to define its objectives by focusing on attendances and seeking expansion. Unless you know, with a fair degree of accuracy, who is visiting your museum already, and what they think of it, it will not be possible to analyse and improve your product, and you will remain ignorant of what motivates your existing visitors. So knowledge of your product and your customers comes first. This is the information which management needs before a marketing brief can be prepared.

The essence of museum marketing is that it should deliver results in an appropriate way. An effective marketing officer can always think of ways to increase customers, but the purpose of a marketing brief is to relate that delivery to the mission statement. In some instances it may be much more important to re-shape the visitor profile than to increase it dramatically - the two activities may or may not be related.

One of the most valuable qualities which a marketing officer can have is the capacity to look at an organisation from the inside and the outside simultaneously. Museum users often have a different perception of a museum to that held by its curatorial staff. They will certainly use a different language to discuss it. During the early stages of creating a strategy, it is vital to view the organisation from the outside, and market research will help you to do that.

A Sense Of Direction

The setting of clear objectives (based upon sound information) is a function of management, assisted by the marketing officer, who is the problem-solver in this situation. Museum marketing and development officers polled in 1991 complained in many instances of the lack of a clear brief from management. A smart marketing officer will be able to think of all sorts of ways, both appropriate and inappropriate, to increase attendances if the brief is that loose. This would be described as becoming 'marketing led'. A clearly thought-out, written down set of objectives will specify which parts of your market you want to expand, with an eye to what kind of service you want to be offering in five or ten years' time, and puts your priorities in the right order.

It may be that you have several different kinds of interface with the public, from all types of visitors, to hospitality users, to people asking for information, and those attending special performances, or members of Friends organisations. Each group of people will need to be considered as part of the plan. Knowing more about your organisation's performance and how it is perceived leads naturally to a recognition of how improvements can be introduced. Then, and only then, can the implementation of marketing take place. There is a whole array of activities which can be brought to bear on clearly defined problems, and plenty of room for creative and imaginative solutions. If ground-work is properly done, marketing can serve you well.

Steps in Preparing a Marketing Strategy

1. SITUATIONAL ANALYSIS

State your organisation's purpose. This will mean setting out the mission statement, exploring its meaning, asking to what extent it is being fulfilled and, if necessary, amplifying it.

The kinds of activities and information which will help you to do this are:

Examination of the Market
Review attendance record
Entry/exit surveys of visitors
Non-visitor surveys
Demographic information about your locality
Information about tourists and tourism policies for the area
Information about public transport services to the venue
Knowledge of any development plans in the area
Access to visitor profiles of other local venues
S.W.O.T. analysis

Examination of the Product
Re-assessment of the displays and programme
Re-evaluation of use of the site
Audit of customer care
Review of human resources available
Review of financial resources available

Examination of Marketing
Describe your current approach.

At the end of this stage, you should be able to assess your current performance against objectives. Where there is a shortfall or room for development you are beginning to specify the requirements of your plan.

2. THE SWOT ANALYSIS

This is an approach which can be used in a number of complex problem-solving situations. Basically it is a way to encapsulate the present

How to write a marketing strategy

2. Hands-on at the Geffrye Museum, London.

situation and anticipate the future, and stands for Strengths, Weaknesses, Opportunities and Threats.

Having gathered the useful information described in step 1 (situation analysis), you can now consider how it fits together. It is often useful at this stage to get a number of different minds working on the problem. A 'think tank' to combine the views of various members of staff may be useful. Apart from gathering a number of different interpretations of the subject, it can be helpful in bringing a common understanding to all members of the team.

However this is handled, the objective is to arrive at a list under each of the four headings. There is a close relationship between strengths and weaknesses. An active body of volunteers may be regarded as a great strength, in offering a pool of assistance. Simultaneously, management of these volunteers may be taking a disproportionate amount of time and effort, which is clearly a weakness. A city centre location may be seen as a natural strength, while the consequent lack of space to expand could be a definite weakness. Strengths and weaknesses are usually related to the measurable properties of the situation, whether they are to do with location of the venue, staff skills, or reputation.

The next pair, opportunities and threats, tend to be a reflection of strengths which have not been capitalised upon, weaknesses which have not been successfully addressed, and factors almost entirely outside the museum's control. For example, the museum may be poorly signposted, which is a weakness, but coupled with a lack of local awareness among non-visitors, a town council's consistent refusal to signpost may have brought an element of threat to future development. Likewise the possibility of achieving better signposting is an obvious opportunity to improve performance. This is also the place to start anticipating future problems or opportunities. Maybe a re-routing of traffic is in the offing, or a pedestrianisation, or the opening of a new theme park nearby. This part of the planning process allows you to consider what are the implications of matters both inside and outside your control.

3. THE MARKETING BRIEF

With all the elements, key questions, trends, performance analysis in your hands, you are now in a position to draw conclusions. In this case, conclusions are only the starting point. What you have done is to identify and isolate the factors which at present prevent you from fulfilling your mission more fully. Only now have you moved into a writing mode, in that you are now able to write a succinct account of your situation, to pick out the key challenges, and to draw conclusions about how they can be met.

At this stage, you will not say exactly how each target is to be met, but you will say what your aims are. For example, you may have discovered that you have a great potential for expanding your visitor base among the elderly, and that a doubling of your existing numbers from this group will go a long way to achieving an overall attendance increase which you seek. The marketing brief will say 'the museum will in particular target the over 60s market, with a view to increasing attendances in this segment by 100% within x years.' This is a very specific target which a marketing officer can respond to by saying *how* this can be done. For reasons which will become clear later, it is a good idea to prioritise your list of objectives at this stage.

4. DESIGNING THE STRATEGY

Each objective identified now needs a strategy to deliver the required results. There are several different tools or processes available through marketing, but at this point you are still thinking strategically. Some further research may be necessary. To return to our example of the over 60s market, it will be a matter of looking at the product from their point of view. Which elements of the visit are most enjoyed by existing visitors from that age group? Which facilities are most appreciated or most lacking? What are the reasons for non attendance in your target market? All this information should already be to hand. You may also know what this group likes to do with its leisure time, what the spending power is, and how significant it is within the tourism market. You may not know much about how they obtain their information about what is going on, where they live, or how they travel. These are gaps which need to be filled. Then you will know what is likely to be an effective way of satisfying their needs and selling them what you have to offer. Now the strategy begins to take shape and, more importantly, can begin to be costed.

At this point, the marketing officer is addressing the question of how to be effective, i.e. by what methods the objectives can be met on time. If you set the budget limits at this stage you will be limiting the solutions offered. This may crush creative solutions, by preventing the exploration of ways and means. Also if you are later going to have to turn down a solution on grounds of cost, you will at least understand the nature of the possibilities on offer, have a good grasp of the priorities you have arrived at, and appreciate the slower delivery rate of cheaper methods (if that is indeed the case). At the end of the day you will have realistic expectations, and if you should decide to try to increase funding for this area, you will know the purpose of the increase and what it is likely to deliver. Failure to work this way round could be one of the greatest hindrances to the growth of effective museum marketing. Planning is all about trying to see just over the horizon, not just up to it.

With a set of costed options, and some clear recommendations from the marketing officer, you should now be able to choose what you can do within a considered budget.

Contents of a Model Brief

- Objectives of the museum with amplification of key points.
- Summary of situational analysis with supporting material, including:

results of market research
information about the locality/catchment area
appraisal of 'competition'
analysis of the product
review of human and financial resources
marketing achievements to date
swot analysis

- Specification of targets for marketing.

The brief might well be a lengthy document, with lots of supporting material, but this is unrealistic where resources are few and problems are well defined. The following is a minimal but entirely acceptable brief which gives a clear steer and would enable the preparation of a plan.

Marketing Brief for Hillside Museum (a fictional example)

- **Objectives of Museum**
  'To preserve and present the Hillside Collection for public benefit.' A programme of collections-care is under way, for which we need increased levels of financial support. The public served has always been predominantly a local one but, with increased numbers of visitors to the area, our Trustees wish to widen the museum's public.

- **Summary of the Situation**
  Results of visitor surveys (to be separately supplied) show that nearly half of our visitors are in the 55+ age group. Organised school groups account for the bulk of the remaining visitors. Teachers express a high level of satisfaction with our education services. 90% of all visitors come from within a fifteen mile radius. 40% of adult visitors have attended at least once previously in the twelve months preceding the survey. A non-visitor survey revealed that most people in the 20–40 age group had not heard of the museum.

  During the past ten years, the small town of Hillside has been developed as an overspill area for the conurbation of Hillstown 20 miles away. The population was swollen by an influx of young families during that period. Tourism organisations show Hillside to be in the catchment area of Hillstown for day excursions. Leisure spending in the area as a whole is on a steady upward trend.

  A country park with limited 'under cover' facilities opened within 5 minutes of the museum last year, and is attracting a larger number of visitors well spread through the age groups. An ambitious shopping mall and car park is due to be built next to the museum within a year.

  A quality of service audit on the museum by an outside consultant (to be separately supplied) shows that shortcomings in our facilities (old-fashioned lavatories, no shop, general dowdiness) is partly compensated for by the friendliness of staff and reputation of the tea-shop. This was borne out by the visitor surveys.

The staff of the museum cannot be changed or increased at present. There is a shortfall in funding of the collections-care programme. No resources are available for improvement of facilities at present. A modest marketing budget may be available. There is no track record in marketing. Main findings of a SWOT analysis were as follows:

STRENGTHS	*WEAKNESSES*
Strong education service	*Lack of awareness among 20-40 age group*
High repeat visit level	*Tiny catchment area*
Collections care programme in place	*lavatories need up-dating*
Good tea room	*Galleries need up-dating*
Friendly staff	*No track record in marketing*
OPPORTUNITIES	*THREATS*
To extend catchment area	*Generation gap among visitors*
To benefit from spending trend	*More income needed to complete collections care programme*
Proximity to country park	*Forthcoming shopping mall*
Offer tea room to country park visitors	
New marketing budget	

Specification of marketing targets, in priority order:

- *Extend catchment area*

- *Increase awareness among younger adults*

- *Improve income generation.*

This brief is very simple. Much more information could have been given, but the essential assets and weaknesses are identified, and the targets clearly identified. The prioritisation is interesting. It must have been a great temptation to put income generation first, but the management of the museum has decided that widening the customer base is more important, perhaps because it will make income generation easier. This prioritisation does need careful consideration. If the response to the brief shows that solving all of these problems is impossible on the resources available, then those objectives lower down the list will be the first to go.

It is also interesting that extending the catchment area is given as a higher priority than extending awareness among younger adults. Again, a hard decision to take. Maybe there is a pragmatic approach here which anticipates that the former will be more cost-effective. Widening the net is likely to be cheaper and give a faster return than trying to break into a new market with possible attitudinal problems. When resources are low, it is usually sensible for marketing to take the line of least resistance. It is a fundamental principle of all marketing that extending a known, appreciative, but unsaturated market is likely to be more cost-effective than creating a new one. In this instance the age group which obviously enjoys the museum is also present outside the fifteen mile radius that defines the existing catchment area. Ability to appeal to younger adults – wherever they come from – is not yet proven. So, instead of trying to change attitudes, the museum is going to try to extend its audience among a group which is already known to enjoy visiting.

Working from this brief, it will be possible for a marketing officer, or whoever is appointed to carry out the work, to look at the possibilities and devise a number of solutions to meet the objecties

Writing the Plan

In the following sections, you will see a wide variety of methods available to the marketing exponent. Later in the book are some case studies which have been selected for their 'real life' qualities. All are tried and tested, and contain elements of success and failure. Most include a varied approach to the problem addressed, choosing a mixture of techniques for their strategic plan.

In the early days of museum and gallery marketing, it is quite usual for management to select one activity only as their means of developing their market. This is the ubiquitous publicity leaflet. It is not surprising that when funds are short and marketing know-how is limited, the introduction of a piece of printed literature may seem all that is required to expand business. When there is no other form of marketing activity, even a maladroit and poorly distributed leaflet *may* make some impact, but it is hardly a considered use of small resources. *Some* level of research is needed; *some* degree of targeting; and *some* thoughtful planning of the distribution.

The function of the plan is to answer the brief; and, in the initial draft, cost will be only a secondary consideration. When an array of methods has been assembled and costed, choices can be made and the revised plan finalised. See the checklist on page 78 for a list of contents which should be included. You may use the A to Z of museum marketing (pages 17 to 79 below) as a checklist on options.

Style

Marketing is a process which, as we can see from the above, is both analytical and systematic. This does not mean that it is devoid of style or creative interpretation. If this was the case, the marketing approach of all organisations would be pretty much identical. In fact style of approach can vary dramatically.

This is because, following preparation of the brief – which must be done in a detached analytical way – the number of solutions will be multiple, and variable. Some will be self-selecting or self-eliminating on grounds of cost. Others will be broadly comparable on cost and anticipated effectiveness. Some may carry an element of risk, others not. Style of management will be the deciding factor, as it is in any other area.

It must be apparent that an ideal situation is one in which there is good interplay between the marketing officer and management, so that each can inform the other and establish an understanding. Marketing officers need to give quick responses and to think on their feet. If they know the character of management thinking, understand the rationale and have a good level of trust established, they will be able to take decisions, carry responsibility and grasp appropriate opportunities as they arise. If they do not, the marketing operation will be lacking in confidence and less effective as a result.

The marketing officer needs to be absorbed into the management team. 'Bolt-on' operations simply do not work. There is now a history of short-term marketing appointments in the museum world. It is all too easy to identify a set of problems which appear to be suitable for marketing solutions, and bring in a marketing officer to 'get on with it'. Managers need to understand why marketing is needed, what makes it work, and be willing to take it on board. Unless a proper examination of the situation and possible strategies are freely and frankly discussed between management and marketing, a rift can open which at best leads to misalignment, at worst to schism.

Consultants can have an important role to play in taking a fresh view, or carrying through an ad hoc task. They are not a substitute for consistent day-to-day marketing practice. This is a symbiotic relationship, in which management policy is translated into practice by marketing but, at the same time, marketing has entered the bloodstream of the organisation.

THE MARKETING PROCESS: AN A to Z

ADVERTISING

Most museums use some form of advertising, usually entries in guidebooks. Such advertising is rarely considered as part of a campaign, still less of a wider marketing strategy. It is simply a baseline activity which is readily available. Some museums have used advertising as a major part of their strategy. The National Museums & Galleries on Merseyside won a great deal of attention with their campaign in the tabloid press, following re-organisation and a bid to win greater attendances. The V&A gained attention by their poster campaign, one part of which featured an 'ace café with a great museum attached.' In both instances the attendant publicity, even controversy, assisted the effectiveness of the advertising, so they cannot be regarded as typical.

The truth of the matter is that museums can rarely afford to buy enough space, and repeat it sufficiently to have real effect. Saatchi and Saatchi advise that museum advertising should always be part of a wider publicity campaign, so that it does not have to work alone, but in concert with editorial coverage and any other publicity which can be gained.

Careful thought is needed before deciding to advertise. It is in many ways the least cost-effective way to promote your museum. Research shows that editorial coverage (articles written by journalists for the news space in a publication) is at least ten times as effective as paid advertising space. This is because readers find editorial more interesting than advertisements, which we have a tendency to scan and skip, and that they are more likely to believe a recommendation in an article than one in an advertisement. But this is not to say that a judiciously placed advertisement will not be effective. Normal rules of marketing apply: the targeting has to be right, in choice of position, publication, and the information presented.

Advantages

- Content is within your control (within the rules of the Advertising Standards Authority)
- You can choose when and where it appears
- It usually takes less staff time than the achievement of unpaid press overage
- In specialist periodicals and carefully selected places it can be narrowly targeted to a specific market
- It complements and enhances other forms of publicity
- If you have a large budget it can be cost-effective in reaching a large number of people.

Disadvantages

- Cost is prohibitive on a small budget
- It is sometimes too broadly targeted
- Design, artwork and production are specialist areas and introduce extra cost
- Its effectiveness is difficult, but not impossible, to measure

Using an agency is usually a good idea. They make money by taking advantage of a discounting system which is not usually open to independent space-bookers. So you lose nothing by booking through an agency, and you may gain, because often they can negotiate better rates. (You should always ask for an educational or charity discount.) The agency may try to persuade you to use their copywriting and design services, which is well worth considering if you can afford it, because this is a specialist area. Having the right advertisement will help your expenditure to work better. If you are considering an advertising campaign it is worthwhile to brief and take presentations from a selection of advertising agencies. Choose the one which shows its understanding of your business through the ideas presented. Sometimes the choice will be difficult, but you will always pick up fresh ideas along the way.

Newspaper and Magazine Advertising

There are two different kinds of space to buy; *classified*, which is mostly made up of small ads in a single column width; or *display*, which consists of larger spaces in specified places. Classified advertising is particularly useful for coming events or for personal appeals for assistance.

Costs may be quoted in column centimetres according to column width. Therefore, a 'ten centimetre double' is a ten centimetre depth by a two column width. Alternatively, it may simply be described as a half page, quarter page, etc. The dimensions quoted are the full extent of the space you may occupy. If you want to put a box around your ad – and it is a good idea to see whether this will help it to stand out from others – the box must fall inside the dimensions quoted. If you are placing a number of similar ads in different publications, it is worth asking your designer to look at all of the space sizes together and decide what is the smallest number of pieces of artwork which can be produced. As a result, you may be able to use two or three original pieces of artwork for five or six slightly differently sized spaces. There is a cost-saving here, although obviously it needs to be done sensibly. Each piece of 'camera-ready' artwork should have the name of the publication and the date of publication written on the back. Strictly speaking, and especially in times of industrial dispute, the designers and/or typesetter's union number should also be written on the back.

3.   *Royal Museum of Scotland, Edinburgh.*

When choosing which publications to appear in, and which part of the paper to appear in, you need to refer to your objectives and your target market. Readership needs to be matched as closely as possible to the kinds of people you want to reach. In specialist publications this is fairly obvious, in newspapers it will depend on the 'slot' or particular space in the paper. Obviously people who go to arts events are likely to spend more time reading the relevant section – unfortunately you have to pay the price for reaching the whole readership, not just the sector you are interested in. This is why events magazines are often so much more effective than daily or weekly newspapers for reaching a visiting public. Your own visitor research will tell you what your existing visitors read, and it is a good idea to take heed of this kind of information.

To find out quantity of readers you can consult the British Rate and Data publication in public libraries, which gives guidance on costs as well. The UK Media Directory also has readership figures, but not costs. Readership is not number of copies sold, but a calculation of how many people read the publication. The life of a publication, and therefore its potential readership is sometimes extended for reasons of timing. Friday and Sunday newspapers tend to hang around the house longer than others, and some magazines sell more copies at holiday times. You are not usually charged extra for this, so it is worth taking into account.

Certain 'slots' in the publication are more noticeable and more often read than others, such as right-hand facing pages, and top and bottom of the right-hand side. You *will* be charged extra for these. It is possible, with sufficient purchasing power, to create your own favoured slot. The Evening Standard, a London daily, has a diary page with a small display ad space at the bottom. Fifteen years ago the advertising agency handling most of London's museum and art gallery advertising recognised that this page was being read by Londoners who wanted to know what was going on in otherwise closed circles. They started to regularly book this space for their clients, and it quickly became a recognised arts/events space. As a result commercial galleries and related companies moved into what had become a 'prestige slot' and soon the price soared with market forces. Now few public museums could afford to advertise there.

If you are asking people to take a definite action resulting from the advertisement, such as making a booking or visiting the museum, you can incorporate a monitoring system by coding each advertisement with a small reference number, such as DT1, for the first advertisement to appear in the Daily Telegraph. Then, if there is an inbuilt telephone contact or a discounting system being used, you can check the reference and see which advertisements are working best for you. It is not always possible to use such a scheme, although once in a while it is worth inventing an inbuilt scheme, such as a competition, discount voucher, or some other way of retrieving the advertisement, just in order to find out which publications are most successful for you.

TV and Radio Advertising

This is not always out of reach. Some museums have found it both possible and effective especially where they use local stations with carefully planned and even more carefully timed small slots. Some of the national museums have been able to take advantage of partnerships with British Rail or London Transport in advertisements featuring different venues. The listener or viewer is not going to be able to respond to complex messages, or remember detailed information, but both TV and radio can be excellent media for putting across atmosphere, the very thing which is so difficult in a printed advertisement.

With the growth of small, special interest radio, it is becoming increasingly possible to target effectively. For example, in trying to reach the Asian community, you may find a station exclusively for that audience. Some stations are particularly good for teenagers. Particular programmes and times of day are right for particular groups. The advertising executives of TV and radio stations will have all of this information at their fingertips. Every 'time slot' will fall into a price band according to numbers of people listening.

Manchester Museum of Science and Industry has advertised successfully on local radio several times. They take small slots at peak times just before public holidays, when people are thinking of excursions. The information content is kept small and brief, while sound effects are used for atmosphere and entertainment value. Attendances are carefully monitored after campaigns, and only if there is a noticeable increase will the advertisements be repeated. By having a flexible agreement, they can monitor weather conditions and decide at the last minute whether extra advertisements will be worthwhile.

There are two sets of costs involved, production and air time. Professional help should be used for both, to get the best out of an infrequent opportunity and to devise an advertisement which may be used time and again.

Transport Advertising

There are a variety of opportunities to advertise in and around transport systems. It can be attractive because people using these systems have to wait for trains or buses, or *in* them, and may be exposed to advertisements repeatedly. You can profitably use their idle moments by giving them something to read. Posters at bus stops and train stations are one method. Purchase of display cards inside buses or tube trains, or 'bus eyes' (the two poster sites on the front of some types of bus) or other shapes of poster on the outside of buses are another way. There are some pitfalls with all of these. It is most unusual for a transport company to sell a single site – although not unknown. You will most probably be looking at a package of sites in various locations on or within the system. (A single site is rarely any use, since all advertising depends upon repetition, and the cost of production for one site would be disproportionate.) This means that the locations within the package need to be examined carefully. It is no good accepting one brilliantly located central site or position, with fifty poorly placed sites at the far end of the station platform on poorly used routes. This is where an advertising agency will help you to assess what you are being offered, and negotiate the best available package. Another potential pitfall is the production cost for 'peculiar' shapes and sizes of site. There is a great deal of standardisation, but while a 'double-crown' site may be a useful size because you can use this large poster at several other display points, some of the more unusual sizes will mean producing posters specially for that purpose and impractical for other uses. This may be an important limitation. Sometimes the opportunity arises to purchase an interestingly positioned individual site or light box (to take a giant transparency rather than a paper poster). For example, you may wish to take a special individual site at your local tube or railway station. This will need careful costing, since production costs could possibly be higher than the actual rental of the site.

Sometimes museums find ways of working together to reduce costs. For twenty years a group of museums in London have been jointly purchasing a particular package of sites on the London underground, and sharing the space according to their requirements and their means. This not only has price advantages, but clusters their posters together and identifies that particular set of sites with a 'what's on' content. Regular travellers begin to build up a familiarity with a particular spot for a particular type of information. Research into tube station advertising in London shows that it is highly cost effective if selectively placed. Millions of people take the same route day after day. During newspaper strikes in the 'seventies and 'eighties, many advertisers moved into tube sites as the only available alternative, and never moved away because of the cost effectiveness.

Design

Design of your museum's advertisement or poster is crucial to success. There are two common failings in design. Firstly, there is a temptation, too often succumbed to, to include too much text. Secondly, when it comes to poster design, there is also a temptation to produce an aesthetically pleasing illustration, which may be artistically satisfying and produce a 'collectable' piece in its own right, but which is not suited to its purpose. A poster is an advertisement, and has to work hard for a living. First it has to arrest people's attention. Then it has to invite action. It may appear on a site where people whiz past within a few seconds, or it may flicker by in the pages of a thick magazine. What is 'eye-catching' is not necessarily the most important or pleasing item in the exhibition or museum. This is where targeting comes in. Who are you trying to reach and what will they respond to? There are some tricks of the trade. Because of our animal origins, we respond immediately to eye-contact. This is why so many magazines use faces on their front covers. Simple, well-defined images will obviously communicate themselves faster than complex or submerged ones. The same applies to text, which should be brief and to the point, giving essential, accurate information. In some rare

4.   *National Gallery of Scotland, Edinburgh.*

instances, such as tube cards, where there is a captive audience, you can afford to use longer text, but not on posters or in most press advertisements.

Housestyle and corporate identity also need to be considered and can work positively for you. Always, the guiding principle must be whether the advertisement will work in the size and the place selected; not whether the image selected is most representative of the whole museum or whole exhibition; not whether the poster is appealing enough to sell in the shop, or to please the curator or artist involved.

BUDGETS

Many museums do not properly identify what they are spending on marketing related activities. What *should* you plan to spend on marketing, and how should a budget be allocated between different activities? Most museums in the UK spend less than 4% of their income on marketing. Both the Museums & Galleries Commission and the Arts Council of Great Britain recommend that the figure should be nearer to 9%. Where admission fees are being charged it is easier to make a purely financial case for a figure approaching 9%. Where a museum is free, it is still important to attract and serve a particular market or markets. Some local authority funded museums where admission is free are encouraged to attract multi-cultural audiences. This can involve major challenges to change patterns of behaviour and attitudes towards museums, and will need funding support to back up the effort. Special exhibitions for the blind and partially sighted will need a special approach to marketing, braille translation, and the funding to support it. So, whether a museum is free or charging, it is the developed mission statement which dictates expenditure. Just because a museum is free doesn't mean that marketing is not required or comes cheaper. In some instances the marketing challenge is greater.

Where admission charges definitely make a difference is in regard to the concept of 'value for money'. Where charges have been introduced in the past decade there has usually been an accompanying investment in services and facilities. Inadequate public lavatories, poor refreshment services and dingy surroundings are seen in a new light when money changes hands at the door. This is a mental perspective which is quite absurd. *All* museums should have decent public facilities. It is a history of underfunding and distorted priorities which have left so many inadequately provided for, and the introduction of charging simply acts as a catalyst for change.

There are three types of funding which need to be taken into account when planning for marketing. The first is money spent on the product itself – good exhibitions, services, facilities and maintenance. If the museum is a dire experience, why throw money at marketing? Word-of-mouth will counteract any marketing strategy. If you have a sound product, which is improving year by year, it is worthwhile investing in marketing. The second call upon your funding is in terms of marketing or promotional personnel – someone to do the work. At present, most museums get by without. If marketing takes place it is often done by a member of the museum staff who 'makes time' for it among other work. This is rarely satisfactory if for no other reason than that marketing is a labour-intensive activity. This in turn means that some level of clerical or secretarial support will be needed. The third need for funding is for a working budget to cover printed material, advertising, and other costs.

Marketing plans are different to individual marketing or promotional campaigns, which vary considerably one from another, but here is an example of a promotional budget for a temporary exhibition which cost £150,000 to mount.

	£ (inc VAT)
Promotional leaflet, two colour, A4 folded, 5,000 copies	1,450
Purchase of specialist mailing list	350
Printing of press view invitation	300
Printing of private view invitation	250
Special size envelopes	100
Printing of black/white photographs for press view	70
Celluloid folders for press kits	20
Two 10cm double advertisements in national press	1,350
Two 10cm double advertisements in local press	380
One 1/8 page Time Out advertisement	375
One 1/8 page local events listing magazine advertisement	55
Additional typesetting costs	120
5 x 30 second slots on local radio for 3 days	1,500
	6,320

Staff time, designer's time, overheads, postage, printing of press releases and press copies of exhibition catalogues are being absorbed here by the museum. In some museums this is no longer the case, and certain items have to be separately costed, such as catalogues. Refreshments at the press and private views should also be budgeted.

The expenditure list above is only the tip of the iceberg. Time is often the major cost of marketing for smaller museums. Staff time will have been taken up with research, policy formulation, copy writing, design liaison, and contract negotiation, before the cash costs begin.

What if the budget is smaller? The above illustration shows a cash budget of around 4% of the overall exhibition budget. About double this amount would need to be spent to achieve the recommended figure. Most museums are in fact spending far less. It is not unusual for a museum to have allocated only a few hundred pounds for all marketing effort throughout the year. How is this arrived at, and how can proper expenditure be justified?

Whether admission free or charging, museum managers need to ask themselves the following questions:

1. Of the public/s described in the mission statement are you attracting/serving them:

    - in sufficient numbers?
    - from an appropriate geographical spread?
    - in the right socio-demographic mix?
    - in the right racial or cultural mix?
    - in an appropriate age spread?
    - well distributed throughout the year?
    - well distributed throughout the week/hours of the day?

2. Are you satisfied with

    - shop/catering/enterprise income?
    - spend per head?
    - public funding income?
    - sponsorship and donation income?
    - your museum's image among your general public?
    - your museum's image among your opinion formers?
    - the marketing component of your forward plan?
    - the marketing mix of your events/exhibitions programme?
    - performance assessment of quality of service?

3. Are you confident that all or most of the above will be answered in the affirmative in two years time and in five years time?

Obviously, if the answer to all of these is 'yes', you have either no need of improved marketing, or are totally self-deluded. If you find it difficult to answer the questions accurately, you probably do not have enough information upon which to base a sound judgement, indicating lack of expenditure on market research.

A half-baked adoption of marketing will rarely be effective. There have been several unhappy grafts of marketing onto unreceptive boards, management or staff. This usually proves to be a costly and time-consuming learning curve for all concerned. The checklist above will help everyone to understand the function of marketing within the organisation, and can become the basis for assessing performance.

- Every museum targeting or achieving over 100,000 visitors a year should have professional marketing help.

- Marketing officers need operational budgets of at least 4% of total income, growing to 9%.
- Marketing is a labour-intensive activity, requiring adequate clerical/ secretarial support.

Having said all this, we do not live in a perfect world, and it is recognised that often a museum manager has to act as the marketing officer in addition to normal duties – or parcel out the work among available staff. The important thing to remember is that marketing is a complete entity, not a bolt-on addition; that it needs resources – around 4 to 9% of income – regardless of who is responsible for it; and that it needs a forward plan as much as any other important element of museum work. Where this publication speaks about 'the marketing officer', it is taken to mean whoever is responsible for marketing, even if he or she has other duties.

CORPORATE IDENTITY

Corporate identity means instant recognition. It conveys the quality of your work, your status, your appeal, to your chosen market. It is more than a logo; it is a style. It is something that can be instantly recognised, and 'felt' or perceived by new members of staff joining the team.

A similar look to all of your printed material, and use of a logo, will blend together all of your activities into a corporate whole. Educational activities, academic publications, special events and other activities will be seen as an integral part of your scope and approach – not as 'extras'. Induction for new members of staff, customer-care training, internal literature will assume a theme which is part of the message for the whole organisation. Museums already have some kind of image within the profession. We are quick to tell one another whether a museum is run along autocratic or democratic lines; whether it has a reputation for innovative work, or whether it's stuck in the mire. Rather than allow these images to evolve accidentally, it can be useful to consider the true nature of the organisation and the kind of museum it is trying to be. If your style reinforces this it will be easier to attract the right kind of staff, and to set the right tone from the start. Potential funders and sponsors will be receptive to a corporate image. It enables you to telegraph your messages rather than keep having to explain who you are and what you are doing. It also looks businesslike, and can help to make a complex organisation more comprehensible.

Complexity is the last thing you want in a logo. Simplicity is the key to success. The organisation which says 'our logo must reflect our diversity – fine arts, natural history, science and social history must all be represented' is going to have a messy solution. If you can refine your character and role, and arrive at a brief which is closer to the mission statement, you will be giving the designer a better chance to think conceptually and devise a unique solution. The woolmark, the simplified skein of wool, is one of the most successful logos ever. This solution may look obvious in retrospect, but there were probably a good few sheep, looms and other paraphernalia in the offing before the final emblem was arrived at.

Sheer repetition can create a memorable logo out of relatively unpromising material. The gold and green Marks & Spencer logo is memorable through mass exposure rather than economy of style. No museum can achieve this level of repetition. Cost is also an inhibiting factor. ICI recently spent well over £100,000 in achieving a minor change in the typographic presentation of their initials. One of the national museums has spent an even higher percentage of its annual turnover in developing a logo. Creativity rather than a Mayfair address is what is needed in logo development. Young, enthusiastic designers can often produce brilliant solutions. The Museum of Science & Industry in Manchester recently achieved a totally new logo, to see them through the next decade or so for £4,000. Highly acceptable results have been achieved by others for under £1,000. Much of the onus is on you to recognise a good logo when you see it.

Here is an outline brief for a logo for a particular museum:

- A logo is needed which will instantly communicate the spirit of adventure in this museum. It needs to reflect its primarily young audience – children and teenagers – and to have a sense of energy or movement.

- The full name of the organisation will usually appear with the logo, and should be considered as part of the design treatment.

- The logo needs to be reproducible in monotone and two-colour printing, and must be legible at the size of a five-pence piece as well as in larger sizes.

- It will commonly appear on posters, leaflets, letter-headings, banners, publications, advertisements, paper and carrier bags, napkins, coasters and paper cups. It may need to be reproduced in floor and wall coverings and installations.

- A full set of guidelines will be required to show how the logo is to be used in relation to paper sizes, letterings, use at top and bottom and side of page, and in conjunction with other logos.

Copies of all existing literature and the freedom of the galleries should then be accorded to the designers, for visual information and inspiration. It is quite normal to ask several design companies to make initial presentations to show how they would approach the task. This can give great insight into how well they understand your thinking before they actually embark on the project. Sometimes they will expect a modest fee for this work, but not always.

Housestyle can go a lot further than a logo or emblem. It really means consistency in style of approach. This can mean anything and everything from how a page is laid out, to colours for captioning or noticeboards, or design of uniforms. This means thinking about details in advance from a logical and practical standpoint. If you stipulate that your logo must always be the same

5.   *Cheltenham Art Gallery & Museum.*

position on a page, you will hit problems with some inflexible future layouts. Considering the alternatives in advance, including the depth of margins, the weight of borders, and other elements which make up the general appearance of your style, will enable a consistency which will give a familiarity to your material without rigidity, and without radical breaks for peculiar formats.

Colour choice also is not a matter of whim. What looks good on paper may not look good in other situations. Consider the plight of a museum which chooses magenta on a letter heading but then wishes to introduce it on wall panels or carpeting within red brick interiors. Does your museum already suggest a range of colours, either through its collections or the fabric of the building? This could be a starting point.

Finally, when you have a logo which is working well for you, the first people to become bored with it are the staff of the museum. Due to their greater exposure to the logo, they (and you) are likely to want to change just as the public are becoming familiar with it. Logos should be changed as infrequently as possible. The time to do so is when market research shows that it is projecting the wrong image, or communicating the wrong message.

DISTRIBUTION

Methods of distributing literature are too often an after-thought. The marketing process starts with research. When sufficient information has been assembled, target markets – the particular groups the museum wishes to reach with its messages – can be identified, priorities selected, style of approach decided upon, and methods of reaching them (distribution) investigated.

Setting aside advertising and editorial coverage, which in a sense are methods of distributing a message, this section deals with the distribution of printed material. The selected method of distribution should have been considered at the time of designing and copywriting the literature. Distribution provides vital information on style and print quantities. For example, if targeting family groups on holiday in the area, one method of distribution will be through the local Tourist Information Centres (TICs). This will mean that the piece of print needs to stand out from a crowd of competitive literature, and will need to be produced in appropriate quantities for the number of outlets. It never has been acceptable, to produce a leaflet loosely aimed at the general public, and then think about how to 'get rid of it'.

Some aspects of distribution are labour-intensive and could be carried out by volunteer or low-paid staff. Stuffing envelopes is not good use of time by a marketing officer or a curator. Needs in this area should be anticipated and provided for as part of the planning process. Similarly, door-to-door leaflet drops, which can be surprisingly effective, except in areas which are bombarded by 'junk mail', should be carried out by volunteers, or even by willing staff on their way home, to an agreed street-by-street plan.

There is a technique in telephone selling called 'cold-calling', where no previous contact has been established, and there is no back-up information to indicate prior interest. This is the hardest and most time-consuming sales technique. It is used where the selling skills are high and there is no more effective method readily to hand. Precious literature should not be used in a scatter-gun effect. There can be good reasons for leafleting local streets, or inserting fliers into local newspapers. Even though the approach to the target market is not tightly focused, the recipients are all within the catchment area and presumably capable of responding to your messages. It is much more effective to use an avenue of approach to groups with an already-established interest in what you have to offer. Thus mailing lists of special interest groups, or readers of special interest magazines, or purchasers of products which have a relationship with your product, are likely to respond in higher proportion than a group approached with a cold-calling or scatter-gun technique.

Some Regional Arts Boards have mail-outs to arts users in the area, so if your gallery is a member and if it is appropriate to your product, this may be useful. Mailing lists can be a good subject for networking or consortia activity, producing more effective lists and cost-savings to each organisation.

It is important to provide copies of your own literature at your own venue. Word-of-mouth is the best advocate for museum visiting, so if you can reinforce a verbal recommendation from a satisfied visitor with an appropriate piece of print, you are assisting one of the most elusive but potent forms of marketing.

A visitor to a nearby venue is a potential visitor to yours. Placing your literature at other museums and tourist attractions is important, but should be part of a reciprocal agreement which is monitored to ensure that it is being carried out as intended. Libraries, bookshops and leisure centres could also be good outlets, and should be similarly monitored.

Performing arts venues often make a charge for interested individuals to be put on a mailing list for programmes of events. The economics involved here do not work well for museums. Selling tickets for a changing programme, at four to twelve or more pounds a seat is a different proposition to offering an events programme which involves only modest charges or free entry. Also, museums rarely run out of products to offer, whereas performances do get sold out, so the customer is motivated by time and supply. Similarly telephone sales are only likely to be of interest to museums in connection with high value sales. For example, telephone selling to previous customers for high value theatre tickets, special offers or season tickets is likely to repay the effort, whereas for modest museum admission charges it is not. Art galleries selling high value art and craft merchandise might well find it worthwhile to use a friendly, personal telephone invitation to previous customers to come in and see a new batch of merchandise. However, the technique is scarcely used, although it works well for commercial galleries with an established client list.

Library services and education authorities often have internal distribution systems for libraries and schools. The museum's education service is probably well aware of these and already using them, but it might be worth exploring additional uses for such outlets, and always worth checking that the style and content is suitable to these very particular markets.

There are commercial display and distribution services, usually based on the major urban centres with brochure display stands in hotels, activity and arts centres. These can be well worthwhile if there is no other way to place your leaflet. Some centres get tired of leaflets 'littering' their foyers, and welcome a properly organised commercial service. Museums which cannot or do not wish to use such a service can often make considerable headway by their own efforts. For example, hotels will often accept literature offered independently or via a tourist board package. Placing and monitoring literature in other venues is a labour-intensive and time-consuming occupation and needs to be built into procedures and routines in the most cost-effective way.

Flyposting is illegal. Many performance venues use it very effectively, since it has an immediacy which can be very attractive to their target market. It is unlikely to be effective for museums except in occasional instances of a special event. Some local authorities turn a blind eye to stickers and small posters slapped onto walls and posts, but some do not. Local authority funded museums would need to think long and hard before trying such a high risk policy.

Compiling your own mailing list is obviously cheaper than buying a list from a commercial source. Running an historical competition or treasure trail, perhaps through a local newspaper, can yield useful names and addresses. Extracting names and addresses from existing visitors is also important, and can be done by offering to put them on a mailing list or send a Christmas catalogue. Evening schools, clubs, societies, disability organisations can all be sources of further information or direct recipients for mailing lists. Assembling this information is a mixture of hoof work and inspiration. Once done, regular 'weeding' is essential. This is usually achieved by sending out a reply-paid card to update names and addresses. (The Post Office business service can explain this system. Only the cards which are actually returned are liable for postage to be paid).

When setting up a mailing list or doing a door-to-door drop, it is useful to work on the principle that like-minded people often live in similar neighbourhoods. We all recognise the estate or housing development which attracts a high proportion of young families. Similarly, there are streets and areas where older and retired people predominate. An existing mailing list of visitors can tell you quite a lot about your customer base, just using the post codes. Through a consortium or Regional Arts Board, you may be able to gain access to ACORN (A Classification of Residential Neighbourhoods) or see recent TGI (Target Group Index) findings. This will help you to understand your market through where they live and what their habits are.

EMERGENCY PLANS

All museums should have well thought-out and well rehearsed plans for what to do in an emergency, whether that emergency is a fire; flood; bomb or other explosion; or a structural collapse; or indeed any other kind of almost unimaginable disaster. There are some good models already in existence, and Area Museum Councils can usually advise, or suggest examples to look at. Dealing with press and media interest, and with any public relations aftermath, is a part of the planning procedure, since it needs to be accommodated at the time, not made up as you go along.

In the midst of disaster, the needs of the press can feel like the last straw. Yet, unless they *are* coped with, their persistence can become a hindrance to the smooth rescue operation. The press have a job to do – even if it seems to cut across yours. Their conduct will become rapidly worse if they are frustrated. The action of coping with their needs makes a positive contribution to events.

If this activity is built into disaster planning, catering for media needs can run alongside the rescue work. People will be delegated to look after journalists and set up lines of communication. Attempted on the spot, all kinds of frustrations are likely to occur; but, planned in advance, advantage can be taken of the opportunities which media coverage can sometimes present. For example, it can show your organisation as a caring institution bringing expertise to bear under stress. Or it can provide a platform for necessary fund-raising to help put things right.

As with every other aspect of forward planning, it requires clear thinking ahead of time on what the real objectives and priorities are. Even more so as events unfold!

We need to consider in advance whether we want the press there; whether they can do a service for us at the same time as our supplying fodder for them; and, if they *are* to be provided for, how this can be done without jeopardising the operation. It is unlikely that a major disaster can be kept secret, even while it is happening. The press monitor the VHF emergency channels to find out where the police, fire and ambulance action is going on. Also, they are known to reward people who tip them off on news stories. So if you want to keep it quiet, the scales are heavily tipped against you. Disasters always catch us unawares, but if your procedures for dealing with them are hostages to fortune, you not only lose the battle, but are seen to lose it in a very public way. The first 12–24 hours following a disaster are crucial not only to the way we handle the disaster, but also to the way we are *perceived* to handle it. Normal procedures require a tree or network of communication to cope with the tasks a disaster prompts. One of the branches of that tree needs to be devoted to media relations. Deciding upon priorities in advance is the key to success.

Since keeping the rescue work free and unencumbered is a high priority, it is sensible to plan for one or two people to have sole responsibility for press relations during the crisis. Responsibility is a key word. If you parcel this work out to anyone less than a capable, fast-thinking, well-briefed member of the team, both they and the press will become a millstone around your neck. There may be moments when this person needs to be tough, as well as supremely tactful, but certainly from the first seconds he or she must inspire confidence in the press that this is someone who can deliver the goods and who understands the journalist's needs. At least one additional helper will be needed to contain the situation and act as a go-between.

The head of operations is going to need to trust this press officer, or acting press officer, if he or she is to delegate authority for important decisions during the crisis hours. This means that free-ranging discussions *must* have taken place beforehand to establish policy on such occasions. If a simple policy exists, and a good understanding has been arrived at, it will take very little time in the actual event for the head of operations to brief the press officer on what is going on and for joint decisions to be taken on press access.

The press officer will need to have made certain preparations in order to have everything to hand at the vital moment. An emergency kit should always be kept ready consisting of one-sentence quotes or definitions worked out in advance, to describe the museum, its collections, and its key members of staff. This is because on such occasions you will probably be dealing with journalists from the 'hard' news team, who do not usually cover cultural or heritage events. They may get your institution's name wrong, and will probably be quite unfamiliar with your collections. To assist accuracy, and help them on the spot, it is as well to give them ready-prepared descriptive phrases. For example: 'The museum houses the country's foremost collection of 17th century furniture', or 'among the best-known exhibits are....'. Also needed will be lists of up-to-date telephone numbers – the Press Association's copy-taking number; key newsdesk numbers; favoured journalists' home and office numbers; and the home telephone numbers of any museum staff or even external experts who may not be expected to be directly involved in the action, but from whom a quote might be useful.

Importantly, the press officer should have been given some prior briefing on conservation first-aid measures and essential techniques. He or she is going to look pretty stupid, and lose the respect of the press, if it's quite obvious that whatever is going on is as much of a mystery to the press officer as it is to the press. Also, it can help to put a proper perspective on the situation if the press officer can give examples of previous damage and describe how in other circumstances the proper care succeeded in saving an object.

So let us look at the mechanics of what goes on. The thing to remember is that the event is only news as it is happening, or in the immediate aftermath. You cannot wait to get a retrospective view of events then present it to the press. You will in all probability have to cope with events as they unfold. This is why you need to switch into automatic responses to the crisis situation.

This is the path of press relations during a crisis. Disaster strikes or is discovered. The head of operations goes into action and, as one of his or her earliest actions, calls in the press officer. If the emergency services are involved, a senior fire or police officer may be in charge of operations. This will alter the circumstances since, if public safety is at stake, this officer may prevent access by the press and take all responsibility for decision-making from your shoulders. In this case all you can do is gather and disseminate information as helpfully as possible, and run on parallel lines to the procedure set out here.

Outline policy on co-operation and objectives will already have been established. If nothing else it saves time. The task of the head of operations and press officer at this point will be to exchange vital information and to look at what access to the scene of the disaster may be granted to journalists. It may be that space is extremely restricted, and that it is only safe for one photographer to be admitted initially. This is a situation with which the press are familiar, and if it is explained to them exactly why the restriction is being made, they can be asked to nominate one photographer who will share material. If access cannot be granted immediately, they need to be told why – and it could be as simple as 'it's not safe' or 'we are setting up a rescue chain' or 'we need to clear debris before you can walk in without further risk to the objects'. But always say they will be allowed in as soon as it's safe, and try to give a time indication, such as 'just a few minutes', or 'we need about half an hour to set up a rescue operation'. Journalists will always want to hear straight from the horse's mouth what is going on, so decide which of the key figures involved can be asked to step aside to give an interview at some point. This may prove very useful if you cannot grant immediate access. Also, you can see that it is important that all members of staff understand the policy and the chain of command in these circumstances. And that this is established well beforehand.

If you are in a situation where the affected area is difficult for journalists to reach, it gives a greater degree of control in the situation, and with historic buildings this is often the case, and can be useful.

What if the emergency services have not been called, because the staff and helpers are coping with the crisis on their own? In this situation, if no one has as yet tipped off the press, you may have the luxury of deciding whether or not you call them in. Bear in mind that if you do not do so, and it really is a disaster, when the news finally comes out, you are going to look as if you were trying to hide something. Also, why deny the public information on the magnificent work that you and your team are doing on their behalf. You may need their sympathy and understanding of the difficult circumstances, and you may need to launch an appeal to raise money for restoration. A fairly free flow of information is more likely to benefit everyone than a clandestine operation. If a more open policy reveals harmful oversights in planning and organisation there is nothing much the press officer can do to save things. Obfuscation leads to exposés later on.

The press officer now has delegated responsibility for handling the press, although there will continue to be information exchange with the head of operations throughout. The first thing to be arranged is an operations base for the press, or at least an information point, ideally with access to a telephone or two. This is not just to contain the press, but to ensure equality of treatment, and to ease practicalities. Even if the whole operation takes place outdoors, a gathering point does need to be established.

A statement will be needed immediately to give available information on what has happened, why and how it happened, or a statement to say it is not yet known how and why, and a brief description of the extent of the damage so far. Most importantly at this stage, every piece of positive information which aids public relations should be given. Some of this might be self-evident, but still needs to be stated. 'The disaster was discovered by staff on a routine patrol, and the emergency services were notified immediately'. 'We have a well-rehearsed procedure for bringing expert assistance to the scene straightaway, and this was put into immediate effect'. Do stress the expertise involved at this point. It helps explain how things happen in a particular and specified way, and commands respect. Also, if you say and emphasise that you have done your duty swiftly and properly, you may forestall speculation and accusations later.

Next you need to give access. This is the best possible evidence that you are working hard to save the situation, and a photograph will tell that story more effectively than anything you say.

The spokespeople you nominate to give interviews need to have been selected on the basis of their level-headedness. An over-excitable reaction at this point might be less than useful. There are also several perspectives on this kind of story. As well as the expert opinions on the nature of the damage and possible remedies, you may find it useful to encourage the human angle. A security person or a cleaner may have been involved in the discovery and may be able to describe the disaster more graphically than others.

It is important to maintain the information-giving role for as long as it is useful, and to monitor how the story is being covered; what if anything is being missed out; and what can be learned for the future.

FUNDRAISING

Strictly speaking, fundraising is a separate activity from marketing. If you are serious about raising money, you should be putting more time and effort into it than a marketing officer can spare from other duties. Given the small numbers of staff employed in most museums it is not unusual for marketing and 'development' to be linked in one job. There is a strong relationship between the two, but both are time-consuming activities, so it must be acknowledged that there is a price to pay for merging the two functions. Even in an ideal situation, marketing will set the scene to support fundraising activities.

A well-marketed museum is easier to raise money for than a poorly marketed one. Newly appointed fundraisers in museums often comment that a low profile is the first thing which they have to tackle in their new job. It is so much easier to open a dialogue with a potential funder or donor if they've heard something about the museum. If they haven't, much of the conversation is devoted to explanations of who, what and where, and then some persuasion about status and importance.

Another connection is that messages need to be similar. If marketing is promoting a museum as a children's venue, for example, the fundraiser will want to swim with that tide rather than against it, and approach funding bodies with an interest in young people. Just as an exhibitions and events programme needs to be drawn up with target markets in mind, a fundraiser's brief needs to be informed by the marketing objectives. This is a case for close collaboration related back to the 'mission' or objectives.

Even well-structured and energetically implemented fundraising campaigns can take two or three years to 'get into profit'. If your museum has a continual need to seek outside funding it makes sense to take a long term view and a steady consistent approach. Relationships with trusts, companies and funding bodies take a long time to establish to the point where communications are swift and easy. It is a common mistake to underestimate the amount of time it takes to foster and see through even a small sponsorship project. This is well worthwhile if it leads to something bigger, but needs monitoring on a time-spent basis. Apart from informing the planning process, management needs to know how much effort is involved in achieving income.

The marketing effort will quite often create opportunities for fundraising, and this is another good reason for sharing information. Every contact made, every parent company of every contact, should be noted and considered from the fundraising angle. It is wise to keep this information on a database (with dated entries), since potentially useful information may become relevant only at a later date.

The following headings form a framework for planning purposes. The order in which they appear relates to their likelihood of repaying efforts with results.

1. Lobbying for increased funding from existing funding bodies.
2. Support from educational and charitable trusts.
3. Sponsorship in cash or goods.
4. Charitable giving/donations.
5. Commercial activity (most museums raise only a small proportion of income in this way).
6. Membership and subscriptions.

GROUP TRAVEL

Success is dependent upon individual museums beating a path to the door of tour operators. Individual approaches are often surprisingly successful. Museums are judged on what they have to offer, and very often seen as unique or 'something different'. Do not be surprised if discounted admission is discussed straightaway. If you have free entry, maybe discounts in shop or cafeteria could play a part, or some extra privilege such as an expert guided tour could be part of the formula. Familiarisation evenings are a useful way to introduce people to what you have on offer. You can organise your own, or if you are a member of a regional tourist board, they will probably be able to help you.

While a tour operator or group organiser may assemble, offer and contract for 'package' holidays, much of the actual booking of accommodation, meals and sightseeing activities is done by a handling or ground agent (sometimes described as an incoming tour operator). There are about 500 such agents in Britain, most of whom will be centred around London. Many are members of the British Incoming Tour Operators Association (BITOA), 120 Wilton Road, London SW1V 1JZ.

Many are tiny, specialised companies. Some will specialise in dealing with tourists from particular countries. Some will handle just short breaks, or budget tours, or speciality tours. There are two ways in which they can affect a museum's business. If they are convinced that the product is likely to be of interest to their customers, they can either recommend to the tour operator that a visit is included, or they can include the museum in the destinations which they book at their own discretion. Itineraries tend to get put together on the basis of well-known venues, or places that customers ask for. If a museum which is not an established attraction is to be included, it stands a much greater chance if it's just around the corner from a major attraction, or en route between one and another – and this needs to be made clear. In fact access and location are most important from every point of view. Minor detours from the beaten track are possible if easy to accomplish and easy to park, but major hikes into unknown territory are far less likely to be included.

If admission to the museum is free, the agent, who is acting as an intermediary and trying to run profitably, may not consider it worthwhile spending the staff time to make a booking, and may either miss out the visit or arrive unexpectedly. Obviously the museum will be attractive to economy budget groups, but it probably will not be the handling agent's first choice. Where there is an admission charge, the agent will expect to take advantage of a group discount.

When it comes to bus and coach group travel, with privatisation, there are now several companies looking at potentially profitable new routes or unusual destinations. An enlarged population of senior citizens means that coach tours are of growing importance for excursions and holidays. Time spent in talking to local coach companies about existing routes and customers will be time well spent. Send them leaflets and offer discounts for groups. Most of all, look after coach drivers by making good arrangements for parking, with clear, well-placed signs and notices. Some drivers will expect a cash payment for bringing groups. Bear in mind that if you start this it will be difficult to stop. Refreshment vouchers might be a better idea.

There are two central organisations which could be useful in distributing information or providing contacts. The National Bus Company is the parent group for 50 local bus and coach companies throughout England and Wales. The Bus and Coach Council is the trade association for bus and coach operators.

6.   *Going down the mine at Beamish, North of England Open Air Museum.*

HELPFUL PUBLICATIONS

Marketing advice can sometimes be obtained from workshops run by Area Museum Councils and other organisations. Fellow marketing officers can usually provide practical advice based on experience. The Museums & Galleries Commission keeps a list of Marketing and Development Officers who have nominated themselves for inclusion. Some regions have museum marketing groups.

Marketing Planning

Marketing the Visual Arts, Arts Council of Great Britain, 1992, £20 (£23.50 including post and packing).

Marketing the Visual Arts : Foundation for Success (Video + workbook), Arts Council of Great Britain, 1989, £15.00 including post and packing.

The Forward Planning Handbook, Routledge, 1990, £14.99 + £2.50 post and packing.

Marketing the Visual Arts : Challenge and Response, Professor Leslie Rodger, Scottish Arts Council, 1987, £5 including post and packing.

Marketing Planning for Museums and Galleries, Gerri Morris, North West Museums Service, 1991, £6 including post and packing.

Implementation

The Principles of Marketing: A Guide for Museums, Association of Independent Museums, £6.90 including post and packing (£5.25 for members).

Managing Consultancy, Rick Rogers, National Council for Voluntary Organisations, 1990, £5.75 including post and packing.

Notes on The Practical Uses of Acorn and TGI Data in Marketing, Arts Council of Great Britain, 1990, free.

Press lists, National and Regional for the Visual and Performing Arts, Arts Council of Great Britain (6 monthly update), £20.

Sample Audience Survey Questions & Guidance Notes on Carrying out Audience/Visitor Surveys, Arts Council of Great Britain, 1992, free.

Low-cost Visitor Surveys, Museum & Galleries Commission, 1994, free.

Tax Effective Giving to the Arts & Museums, Arts Council of Great Britain, 1990 and 1993, £6.50 including post and packing.

Computers for Arts Marketing, Michael Prochak, Arts Council of Great Britain, 1992, price on application.

TGI National and Regional Summaries, provided by the Arts Council of Great Britain free to ACGB and RAB clients.

The Results of Research Into the Contemporary Visual Arts, Arts Council of Great Britain, 1992, free to ACGB and RAB clients.

Museums and Tourism, Museums & Galleries Commission and English Tourist Board, 1993, £5.50.

Quality of Service : Customer Care in Museums, Guidelines on Implementation, Museums & Galleries Commission, 1992, free.

Customer Care : Peripheral or Essential? Carnegie United Kingdom Trust, 1992. £8.95 (£10.95 inc post and packing).

Arts Funding Guide, Anne Marie Doulton, Directory of Social Change, 1992, £14.95 + £1.50 post and packing.

A Guide to Major Trusts, Directory of Social Change, 1992, £14.95 + £1.50 post and packing.

A Guide to Company Giving, Directory of Social Change, 1992, £14.95 + £1.50 post and packing.

Guidelines on Disability for Museums & Galleries in the United Kingdom, Museums & Galleries Commission, 1992, free.

Touch in Museums & Galleries: selective bibliography obtainable from the Arts Officer at the Royal National Institute for the Blind.

Disability Design Museums. Proceedings of joint seminar of GDIM and MAGDA obtainable from Secretary of Museums and Galleries Disability Association, c/o British Museum Education Service, Great Russell Street, London WC1 3DG.

ABSA/WH Smith Sponsorship Manual, Association for Business Sponsorship of the Arts, £7 including post and packing.

Principles for Good Practice in Arts Sponsorship, ABSA, £3 including post and packing.

ABSA/Arthur Anderson Tax Guide, ABSA, £3.50 including post and packing.

The Acorn User Guide, CACI Information Services, CACI House, Kensington Village, Avonmore Road, London W14 8TS. Price on application.

Can I Quote You on That? Frank Albrighton Conference of University Administrators, 1986, £1.

The Handbook of Public Relations, Ylva French, The Museum Development Company, 1991, £24.95 (£27.95 including post and packing).

Cultural Trends (Yearly), Policy Studies Institute, £15 per issue.

The Museum Trading Handbook, Hilary Blume, Charities Advisory Trust, 1987, £7.95.

Lobbying : An Insider's Guide to the Parliamentary Process, Alf Dubs, Pluto Press, 1989, £10.95.

Gift Aid : A Guide for Donors and Charities, Inland Revenue (IR 113).

INCENTIVES

The difficulty of introducing incentives to an admission-free museum has already been touched upon. But this is a challenge rather than a closed option. An incentive can take many forms; it is simply a promotional tool to encourage greater use of the product.

When admission charges apply, discounts can be used in a number of ways to shape the museum's business. For example, cheaper entry at quiet times of the day, week or year may encourage more visitors to come – if properly promoted. If it is intended to increase business overall, rather than to redistribute it throughout the year, it needs to be carefully structured, possibly in the form of vouchers for two or more people visiting together, or linked in a repeat-visit offer. Sometimes, in situations of frequent overcrowding at peak times, it might be useful to use incentives to encourage people to come outside those hours. For example, if the British Museum decided that it had become critical to redistribute visitors away from peak hours, and if they charged admission, they could ensure that there were significant savings to visitors in the quiet times, and perhaps a positive disincentive in the busy hours. Since they do not charge, they might take the same principal and apply it in a different way. For example, discounts could apply in shop or refreshment areas, or special features – free guidebooks, tours or demonstrations – could be offered. Or it could simply become the theme for a publicity campaign, to promote the charms of viewing at quieter times. Museums rarely do this – indeed they rarely ever give guidance in their information literature, as to best and worst times to come. The effective solution is probably a combination of several or all of these measures.

The timing and targeting of an offer is important. Offering a free repeat-visit voucher to group travellers who have come from a long way away is something of an empty gesture. Visitors from nearby are as likely to hand the voucher on as use it themselves. While this may help to extend audiences, it will be even more effective if it is given on the basis of one person free to one paying; or children free with paying adults.

Your incentive may take the form of a free gift – especially if you can find a sponsor, or a company to donate goods. This will have to be clearly described as a limited offer. An example of this would be an offer for the first 100 children into a special exhibition to receive a badge. This will help to get things off to a good start, and will be talked about.

Advance sales of tickets for special exhibitions at a specially discounted rate are an appropriate incentive rarely used by museums. The Royal Academy is now in the business of advance ticket sales, and has proved that it can work

7. *National Waterways Museum, Gloucester.*

well. They have obvious advantages of reputation and location but, where they have led, others are beginning to follow. As museums learn to work more closely with the travel industry, this is likely to become more of a feature. Long-term planning, publicity and early decision-making over prices are obvious requirements.

Privilege is a kind of incentive, and can be used to develop Friends groups. In this case, access at unusual times, previews, priority booking offers, and special talks and introductions are likely to be some of the incentives on offer. Special offer discounting of admission entry plus catalogue is a possibility which could be offered to Friends and public alike.

Competitions are a kind of incentive. If you have branch museums you could structure the competition to require visiting more than one site. If you wish to organise a prize draw for which tickets are sold – rather than being based on skill or lucky guess – you will need to buy a licence. Forms are available from local authority offices. The National Lottery is to benefit museums, and there may be opportunities for museums to act as licensed agents for selling tickets.

Another use of the word incentive appears in relation to incentive travel. This is an important and growing market in the UK. It is an increasingly popular system of company reward for excellence. The best sales team, the most successful branch, or the brightest ideas might be rewarded by a weekend in a pleasant area with specially arranged visits to interesting venues. Over £1 billion is spent in the UK each year on this kind of 'bonus'. Financial rewards can be high, but organisation needs to be impeccable. Specialist travel operators are usually responsible for setting up the arrangements, and their advice is essential for delivering the rather exacting requirements of this market.

JOINT SCHEMES

Working together with other organisations is often a good way to extend markets and share costs. By its very nature a joint scheme will be the result of a group or committee taking decisions together; so, before you set out, you need to have considered your institution's individual objectives very carefully and stated them clearly to the other members of the group. This will make it easier to measure the usefulness of proposed courses of action as you go along, since joint action is more likely to get complicated than become simple.

Joint ticketing is a prime example of the type of difficulty which can be encountered. A group of venues may decide that by selling a single ticket, or passport, to all their sites, they will each win extra visitors from the others, and that this will benefit everyone. Naturally, a discount of some kind needs to be involved in order to incentivise the purchase. This immediately brings the ticket outlets into extra administration costs, since income will need to be divided. Paperwork, proof of purchase and bookkeeping suddenly present an extra burden, and one which may not be evenly distributed between sites.

Tourist boards often voice their enthusiasm for museums to offer a passport scheme which would enable tourist board offices at home and abroad to offer tourists 'the freedom of our museums'. To make such a scheme work, a very substantial proportion of museums in a given area would need to participate. Some are free; some are independent, some have to make returns to local government or to a wing of the armed services. Thus the financial structure would need to be very complex in order to cope. Such schemes are possible, but need a clear-thinking, practical approach and sometimes an acceptance that the offer, because of its administrative expense, is run as a public service rather than a profit making venture.

Some museum consortia have found that simply working together for information-giving, publicity-seeking purposes is much more manageable. The museums of the Yorkshire and Humberside regions do this very successfully, and they are one of the case studies included in this publication.

Sometimes teaming-up with non-museum organisations can make a lot of sense. Helping a local hotel to create themed weekends or special breaks can provide long-lasting benefits. Local bookshops, craft shops, garden centres, etc may be pleased to feature promotional material based around an exhibition on a subject which allows them to promote their products alongside.

As well as major campaigns involving tourist boards and other partners, there are sometimes smaller opportunities. A publisher or manufacturer launching a new product with some relevance to an exhibition or part of the collection may be persuaded to hold the launch at your museum. The venue is likely to be seen as something of a novelty, and you will have an opportunity to benefit from resulting publicity. Naturally, you will make a charge for the use of the premises, unless some tangible benefit is being offered. So, while this is an area for experiment, you will need clear objectives and monitoring of costs and time resources as you go along in order to find out what benefits you can gain. Goodwill and proximity are insufficient reasons for joining forces with other organisations. There has to be a proper examination of existing markets, and of what each partner hopes to achieve. Once a way of working together can be found, many things may suddenly become more practicable for the group than for the individual organisation. Tourist boards are likely to be interested in joint schemes. Together, your purchasing power may be enhanced. Requests to well-known personalities to make appearances may carry more weight. In fact, you may be taken more seriously in a number of useful ways.

KNOW YOUR MARKET

Even if you have no intention of introducing a marketing strategy for your museum, you do need market research. If you intend to market the museum, surveys of visitors are the building blocks of all future work. In the 1970s the Natural History Museum started to survey its incoming visitors. The results were salutary. They had always believed that their visitors were particularly interested in the natural sciences. Their research showed abundant curiosity and a desire to find out about things in an amusing way, but only a tiny fragment of their visitors had studied biology to 'O'level, and most had no more than an average interest in natural sciences. This affected the way in which every label, theme and message was presented, from that moment on. Suddenly they knew who they were talking to, and began to develop much more effective ways of doing so. Market research is now a regular feature of their work. As a result, when planning an exhibition about mammals in the late 1980s they first made sure of what most people understood by the term, and used it as their starting point.

So market research can simply be a way of getting to know your audience in order to devise a form of communication which works. It doesn't mean coming down market. It means using an appropriate language, finding the right starting point to enable you to 'connect' with your visitors, and probably to fulfil your mission statement. Art galleries are often poor performers in this area, since their audience often seems to come to gaze in awe, and probably departs without having communicated their lack of enlightenment. As a result, it is tempting for curators to suit their own standards and expectations, or those of vocal art critics, rather than suiting the majority of their visitors. Working in a vacuum is fraught with danger.

Sometimes market surveys can reveal pleasing surprises. One local history museum had assumed that its visitors were largely made up of a core of the same local people visiting again and again, but they discovered a significant minority of first-time visitors from just outside their assumed catchment area. This encouraged them to promote the museum more widely, but into areas where they knew there was already some level of interest. This is how market surveys can assist planning in marketing.

Cost effective marketing, rather like water, always takes the line of least resistance. It is difficult and expensive to create a new market, and much easier and cheaper to expand an existing one. Sometimes mission statements and accompanying museum policy may dictate that new and difficult markets must be won – perhaps minority groups of some kind are not served by the museum as much as they should be. It is not possible to switch a fixed amount of effort and resources from one area to another and expect the same amount of return, so the character and difficulty of the target market must be considered beforehand, and budget decisions made accordingly. But unless the original research is done, and evaluation carried out, you will never know your starting point or your success rate.

You can find out a certain amount about your potential market by looking at research which has been carried out in other sectors. Your local authority will know certain things about people who live in the area, from numbers to age groups. They should also be able to say how the population is expected to change and re-structure in the foreseeable future. This is information which they need for planning purposes. National demographics are worth looking at to discover the same sort of information. Are the same number of

8. *Ulster Folk and Transport Museum, Northern Ireland.*

schoolchildren going to be in school in the next decade? Does the increasing number of elderly and disabled people have any impact on your future plans? If there is a boom or a recession, are certain groups experiencing the effects more than others?

Sometimes the results of surveys are published, and it may be possible to get access to them, either through newspaper or magazine reports, or through the good services of local tourist boards, regional arts boards and area museum councils. The Arts Council gathers information about arts-going habits through questions added to the Target Group Index. All this information paints a general picture of an available market. To find out how this relates to your museum, it is essential to carry out your own market research.

There are very few cheap effective ways of doing this. Sometimes you will be lucky in persuading a local college with a business planning, statistical or marketing course to join forces with you to conduct a survey. The learning curve will be pretty steep on both sides, and it may not answer all your requirements. Some museums have conducted their own modest surveys with mixed results. The most common mistake is grossly to underestimate the input time, even when using specifically designed databases. Self-completion questionnaires seem like a short-cut, but if people are not encouraged and motivated, person-to-person, it can take a long time to achieve sufficient numbers. There really is no satisfactory alternative to spending *some* money on a professional survey.

The basic things you will need to discover are:

- age groups
- occupation
- distance travelled
- method of travel
- solo or part of a group
- frequency of visits
- other venues recently visited.

There are many other things you will want to find out, including motivation, how they first heard of the museum, what they read; and, if doing an exit survey, how long they spent in the museum and what they enjoyed most and least.

There are questions which it is unwise to ask during a visitor survey, no matter how tempting. These are questions which prompt a polite response rather than an honest one, and ones which ask people to solve problems in specialist areas. Visitors co-operate with surveys because they are willing to help the museum, as long as they are not detained for too long. The interview usually takes place in an atmosphere of goodwill towards the museum, so they are not generally inclined to give over-critical responses. A general instinct to be polite is going to make their replies a bit more favourable than if they were simply discussing the museum among friends. Therefore asking them if they intend to visit again is a waste of a question, unless you are simply collecting material for propaganda purposes. It is far more to the point to ask if they saw everything they wanted to see during their visit; whether anything was missed. This politeness factor needs to be taken into account when assessing results of an on-site questionnaire.

Other wasted questions are 'how much would you be prepared to pay if there was an admission charge', 'what should we sell in our shop', 'what additional attraction or service should we provide?' These are open-ended to a ridiculous degree, and can only obtain hypothetical answers based on the individual's conceptions and misconceptions of your business. These are the answers which you must discover through better knowledge of your visitors' existing spending patterns, likes and dislikes.

The research discussed so far is all quantitative, in that it results in numerical information, with some comparative material, and some comments in peoples' own words resulting from open-ended questions. Another kind of research is qualitative, resulting in a more detailed picture of how your organisation is perceived. It can be a good way to test new design ideas or suggestions for future developments.

The usual format for qualitative research is the use of focus groups. These are representatively structured discussion groups of about eight people lead by a facilitator. It is a method for discovering attitudes through the way people talk. Although this can be done by you with the aid of various helpful books and guidelines, it will be much better done by a professional who understands how to compose the group, and how to get the most reliable information out of the discussion.

Having carried out the research, don't let it gather dust. You need to extract the maximum amount of useful information. If a consultant has carried out the work for you, have an agreement from the start that they will help you to interpret the information once gathered. Initially, you are looking for groupings. You need to know whether there are clusters of common interest, habits, age groups, motivations. In doing so, you are beginning to identify your target markets.

LITERATURE

The first marketing step which any museum or gallery takes is usually the production of a piece of printed material for promotional purposes. While it may not be possible to produce a promotional leaflet for every target group you are interested in, it is essential even if writing one for 'general use', to consider beforehand the methods of distribution available, and to imagine the recipient as a reader who needs to be motivated. Printed material looks like evidence of marketing activity, but needs to be just the visible part of a larger, well-structured underlying approach.

Before embarking on a programme of print preparation and production, it is advisable to consider whether this is indeed the vehicle needed to get your message across. Have you ever researched the effectiveness of your printed material? Or perhaps a similar organisation has done so, and is prepared to share the results with you. The Ikon Gallery in Birmingham began to have serious doubts about whether the posters produced to accompany each exhibition were actually effective. As an experiment, they withdrew posters, but continued normal publicity efforts to get coverage in the press. Visitor figures remained unaffected, so they deduced that it was not always necessary to have a poster for an exhibition. It can be useful to question existing assumptions from time to time.

In order to establish whether or not you need printed literature, consider the target group you want to reach and think about the best way to reach them. For example, if you are trying to reach a teens and twenties age group, are leaflets the best way to do so? It may be that editorial or advertising in favoured magazines would be more effective. Maybe you have the right experience in-house, or maybe you will need outside help. This all comes back to budget. If overwhelmed by the amount of things you want to achieve on a small budget, remember that it is always better to have limited objectives which can be fulfilled, than trying to spread resources too thinly and failing on all fronts.

It is not possible to make recommendations as to how much and what kind of literature any museum should have. It will vary with each museum and its target markets.

The sorts of literature you might consider are:

- A tourist leaflet for use in TICs
- Fliers for insertion into magazines, newsletters, or mailings
- Posters
- Direct mail letters
- Newsletters/events programmes
- Special leaflets on individual exhibitions/events
- Pro forma letters or information sheets.

There are many more, of course, from invitation cards for opening events, to special approaches for special markets – such as braille leaflets or sound tapes for the visually impaired.

Once it has been decided that printed material is needed; what kind is needed; what system of distribution (and therefore what quantity) is needed; it is then advisable to draw up a production schedule, if the literature is to be produced on time. The smart thing to do is to handle printed material which needs to look integrated – such as all print material for an exhibition – together, so that there is an economy on production of logos, plates or typesetting costs. Considerable savings can be made if a designer is working on advertisements, leaflets, invitation cards, posters, special press release papers, all at the same time. Also it is easier to develop a similarity of style for each piece of print.

To establish your schedule, work back from the required launch date. When is the optimum time to send out invitations, leaflets, posters? When you have worked out how much time you need to sort and distribute material, you can arrive at a required delivery date. (It is wise to work slightly ahead of deadlines in order to absorb delays or cope with problems along the route. Keep this contingency reserve to yourself. Once suppliers know you are using false deadlines, you will be into games of double bluff and in danger of losing touch with reality!)

Still working backwards, allow time for printing, according to the size and complexity of the job. Time will have to be allowed for one or even two opportunities to read proofs and check layouts. Colour accuracy may be extremely important if you are producing a work of art, so allow time to check colour proofs carefully against the best available material, and if necessary ask the printer if you may check the first print as it comes off the machines, (a small amount of adjustment to the quantities of ink can be made at this stage).

When working with printers, it is useful to bear in mind the old adage, that if it can go wrong it will go wrong. What this means is that you should be prepared for the worst to happen all along the way, then you will be pleased if it goes smoothly, and calm if it goes wrong. Some examples of the pitfalls:

- bits of pasted-up text falling off artwork
- sole copies of text/proofs/photographs getting lost in the post
- binding going wrong, so that pages appear in the wrong order, or twice
- registration going wrong, resulting in blurred printing or peculiar positioning
- artwork being wrongly measured, so that text disappears into the binding
- mental blackouts among copywriters, resulting in 'Tuesday 22nd instead of Tuesday 23rd'
- forgetting to include the time and place
- unique colour transparencies getting trampled on the printshop floor (scratches on the shiny side can be professionally removed; those on the emulsion (less shiny) side cannot).

All of these, and more, and worse, have happened to the author. The safeguards you can use are as follows:

- keep copies of everything
- create quiet time to proofread with a colleague who is unfamiliar with the text
- check everything at all stages
- leave time in the schedule to correct mistakes
- work with good printers (not necessarily the cheapest)
- work with intelligent designers
- have a simple contract with the printers, and make them correct mistakes which are their fault.

Continuing to work back from the stated delivery date, work out how long the designer will need to design and layout typesetting. Think about how much discussion will be needed before a design is approved, and allow time to brief the designer fully about what kind of job is needed, and who it is aimed at.

Working back from there, you can calculate how much time is needed for copywriting, assembly of illustrations and credits or acknowledgements. Maybe the draft will have to be approved by someone else (or a committee), so allow time for that.

It pays to familiarize yourself with certain terms used by designers and printers. This will help you to understand them, and make it easier to clarify exactly what you want. Here is a selection:

Paper sizes: You are probably familiar with A sizes. This is the international system based on the A1 size of 841mm depth by 594mm across. Fold this in half, and you have A2; in half again for A3, and so on. A popular leaflet size is A4 folded in three. This you will hear people speak of as 'third A4 size', which is handy for people's pockets and most forms of brochure display, measuring 99mm x 210mm. Envelope sizes relate to A sizes. Most printers will be happiest working in A sizes, since it enables them to get the most economical cuts from the paper they use. Once in a while, often when working with publishing houses or advertising agencies, you will hear other sizes mentioned, such as demi-octavo, jumbo or elephant. Always ask for exact sizes in millimetres or examples, so that you can see for yourself.

Dummy: This is not a term of abuse, nor something to suck in moments of anxiety, but a good starting point for any material where folding is involved. By producing a mock-up, you can work out where each piece of information or illustration should appear, so as to read logically when folded or opened up. 'Printers latin' – a nonsense text to simulate spaces where copy will appear – is often used in dummies or mock-ups.

Binding: The way in which pages are joined together at the spine. Saddle-stitched usually means stapled in two or three places. Perfect-bound means that glue is used to achieve a flat spine, which is useful if you want to print the title on the spine for better visibility on bookshelves.

Half-tone: Instead of solid colour, you may wish to achieve a fainter or paler version. This is done by increasing or decreasing the dots of colour used, and can best be seen by looking closely at photographs in newspapers, where the dots are easily seen. (Incidentally, you cannot use a photograph taken directly from a newspaper and reproduce it by another dot matrix system. The registration of the dots is impossible to achieve, and you end up with a blurred effect. Another negative must be made, or the original photograph obtained). The density of a half-tone is expressed as a percentage tint. Thus an 80% half-tone is nearly solid colour, while 20% is a fainter, paler version. Using a half-tone provides variety without having to pass the paper through the presses for a second time – for example black and grey can be printed at the same time, and red and pink. This saves costs. Some lithographic printers can offer 'colour merge', which allows several colours to be printed at the same time. It can be very effective, but may not suit reproductions of works of art.

Offset Litho:	The commonest form of printing for posters and leaflets. A colour separation is made, to produce a separate plate for each colour, and this can be a high proportion of the cost of printing. If the job is fairly straightforward and simple, a designer can do the separation at artwork stage. Screen printing is a method for larger pieces of print where small quantities are needed. Process printing is the full-colour method of printing colour photographs, using computerised scanning equipment for the colour separations.
Artwork:	A misused and abused term, with only one correct meaning. It is the final product of the graphic designer's work, providing 'camera-ready' text and colour separations mounted on board, with full instructions to the printer. Never treat artwork casually; check it very carefully with clean hands; and get it back from the printer to keep for a while in case of need.
Reversed-out:	Instead of printing words or images in solid colour, the space around them is printed, leaving the paper to show through.
Art paper:	A smooth paper which is good for photographs. Coated papers can be even better, depending on the style you are aiming for. The weight or thickness of a paper is measured in grammes per square metre (gsm). Only go below 135 gsm if the designer assures you it will work, or if it is specified by the end user. (Posters to be pasted onto hoardings sometimes have to be of a particular thinness). Textured papers are usually more expensive, but can upgrade the look of a job, especially if only one or two colours are being used. If using recycled paper, be sure to print a note to that effect somewhere on the job. People like to see this kind of

awareness, especially in material which could be classed as 'throwaway' or junk mail.

Pantone colours: A comprehensive colour system which ensures consistency. Full Pantone swatches are usually held by designers, but a good selection of colours are shown in the letraset catalogues. 'Standard' colours are cheap because they are ready-mixed. Black is usually cheapest of all.

PMT: This is a crisp, highly defined, densely printed original print, usually used for logos which will need to be produced on a large number of different jobs. A clear photocopy is not a substitute.

Whatever kind of printed literature you are considering, always remember what it is intended for and be sure to include essential information to enable readers to act upon your message. For instance, as well as the title of an exhibition, you need to give dates, times, location and price. In leaflets a small map to show exactly where you are can be a good idea. Also, keep one or two samples of everything you print for future reference and consistency of style.

MONITORING/EVALUATION

It is essential to measure effectiveness whenever resources are being used. This is not just a management inspection device, it is a way to learn more about your business and do better in future. Understanding mistakes can be particularly interesting since sometimes mistakes can tell us more than success about how to communicate with our markets. Some areas are more difficult to measure than others. Inbuilt devices that the public can scarcely detect are usually more effective than questioning the public directly. It is difficult to underestimate the capacity of people to remember what motivated them on some occasions. The first Fabergé exhibition at the V&A prompted queues which snaked down the Cromwell Road. Those queuing were asked what had prompted them to come, and what they thought the exhibitions was about. This is just a sample of the answers given:

'I read about it in the Times' (no article had appeared).

'I saw the advertisements in the press' (no press advertisements had appeared).

'I saw the queue and joined it'

'It's all about perfume' (Fabergé 'Brut' advertisements were appearing at the time).

'It's all about chocolates'.

Time and again, public recall proves unreliable. More precise methods are needed.

Advertising: a notoriously difficult area to evaluate. If you are asking for a response via the telephone, by use of vouchers or coupons, or booking forms which form part of the advertisement, you can number or code each ad, so that the responses can be measured and compared. For museums, this is rarely possible. Large retailers have exactly the same problems. Sometimes the only way that effectiveness of advertising can be measured is to withdraw it from one particular medium and see if sales drop. This is not practical or reliable for small-scale museum advertising.

Budgets: naturally expenditure needs to be monitored, and can be reviewed on a regular basis. The results of evaluation should be fed into the annual budget review, since they will be helpful in deciding priorities for next year.

Corporate Image: focus groups are the best way to find out about your corporate image. Remember, if you are getting tired of it, it is probably just beginning to register with the public – but test it.

Distribution: if you use more than one method of distribution, it is a good idea to compare their effectiveness from time to time. Including an entry form for a quiz, competition, or money-off voucher in your literature, coded differently for different outlets, can show you which method is bringing in most customers. Such an exercise needs meticulous stock control or the results will be worthless.

Emergency plans: new fire regulations, becoming fully effective in 1996, require you to have plans, staff training, and rehearsals. Do have post mortems after rehearsals, and listen to staff comments. The only way to find out how effective you are is for the real thing to happen; then it's too late to improve. Do read National Trust accounts of what happened at Uppark, and English Heritage accounts of what happened at Hampton Court. Ask curator colleagues to consider whether they would rather have prize objects smashed by being thrown out of a window, or consumed by fire. Some level of mental preparation may help decision-making under pressure. Fire and safety officers can help to monitor the effectiveness of evacuation procedures during drills simply by observing and reporting back.

Fundraising: tends to be a self-monitoring area. Targets are usually set too high in the first three years. The appointment of a first fundraiser usually has more effects and benefits than just the cash raised. It is only fair to note and evaluate assistance with forward planning, developing new attitudes and approaches, and public relations services which are also involved.

Group Travel: it should be easy to collect information about where groups have travelled from. Once in a while it can be instructive to mark the areas on a map. See how they cluster and where the gaps are. Ask why, work it out, and use the results to extend business. Talk to coach drivers about what people say they enjoy most.

Joint Schemes: since these sometimes take an inordinate amount of energy to organise, and because cost is involved, and inevitably the question will arise of whether to repeat next year, it is a good idea to build in some system of evaluation which will enable you to decide whether it was worthwhile for you.

If ticket sales are involved there should be opportunity to do this; if not, market research is probably the only way.

Literature: It is difficult to evaluate every piece of literature you produce, but once in a while you may want to test an individual item, or look at reactions to a particular approach. Focus groups are probably the most useful way to do this.

9.   *National Museum of Wales, Cardiff.*

Monitoring/evaluation: from time to time it can be useful to have a fresh eye cast over the systems you use. Maybe you can compare notes with another similar museum, or bring in a consultant for some ad hoc work.

New Markets: Keep track of your costs in creating new markets, and look closely at the results in market research. Are your campaigns working? What is it costing you per new visitor? Is it worthwhile?

Opinion-forming: by their very nature, the opinions of opinion formers are hard to get at. If you are increasing your contact with key people you will get a fair idea of what they think as you go along.

Press relations: performance in this area used to be measured in column inches solely. Quantity of coverage is an indication of activity with results, but coverage gained should always be looked at in relation to the targets aimed at. Are items appearing in the parts of the press you particularly want to reach? It is also wise to take a long-term view, especially if you have complex messages to get across. Are key press turning up consistently for your press events? Do you get called for a quote if there is a relevant story going on? Are you able to give more complex messages to journalists with whom you have fostered a relationship? These may be more important signs of progress than column inches, desirable as they are.

Quality of Service: monitoring is the key to achievement in this area, and should be a regular feature of your operation. Researching, identifying, and deciding upon your own performance indicators is the best policy, but ideas can be gathered from the National Audit Office 1993 report on Quality of Service in Five National Museums.

NEW MARKETS

Almost invariably, new markets are harder to win than extending existing markets. There are several reasons for this:

- you cannot apply knowledge gained through experience
- starting from scratch is more challenging than building on what you already have
- there is usually a good reason why that market has not been won already.

There are two reasons why you might believe that, despite the difficulties, you should venture into new markets. First, you might realise that it would be a financial advantage to attract a particular group, or more of a particular group, because you want to persuade them to become Friends or donors. Second, it would help to fulfil your mission statement, because they are a group which should be served by the museum. Sometimes it will be a combination of these two reasons. Whatever the motivation, it is important to be aware of the resource implications such a decision carries.

Let us take, as an example, one decision to target a particular group of disabled people, those with impaired vision. This is a group to whom many museums feel a particular responsibility, since so little has been done to make collections accessible, but where it has the results have been dramatic and appreciated. Targeting blind and partially-sighted people is not simply a matter of extending mailing lists. The key to working this area is an appreciation of how long it takes for information to filter through the chain of communication to the point where action is taken. Publicity has to start far earlier; exhibitions need to run for longer; talking newspapers need to be researched and accessed; busy, pre-occupied radio programmes need to be persuaded that this topic has sufficiently high priority – and to broadcast early rather than late; sighted helpers need to be targeted through normal channels of approach in time to arrange assisted group travel; and, because of general mobility problems, more time needs to be allowed for word to get around and action to be taken. All of this has cost implications.

Another common 'new' market are ethnic groups who rarely enter the museum. There are some interesting thoughts on this in 'Could do Better' published by the West Midlands Area Museum Service. There is usually a reason why people of a particular racial group or different cultural background do not come to their local museum. It may be that museum-going is simply not part of their leisure habit, or that they feel the collections are irrelevant, or the atmosphere unwelcoming. There are big challenges to meet, because real change must be brought about. This is more than a promotional exercise. The resource implications are likely to be pressures on time, since much research and contact-making will be needed, with good internal communications allowing staff to explore issues which arise.

The same holds true whether you are trying to move your visitor profile up or down market. You need to discover preconceptions and resistance, and then

10. *Press clippings from a time of crisis. Is all publicity good?*

work to put it right. This is a prime example of how marketing needs to intersect with every other aspect of museum activity, from public services to exhibition planning. New markets cannot be won without a co-ordinated approach.

OPINION FORMING

People who don't work in museums understand very little of what goes on inside a museum, and probably have not given much thought to the subject. It is more than likely that the ideas which they do have are quite wrong or out-of-date. Try asking. A picture will emerge of dusty treasure houses; a cloistered hush; curators who spend their days turning interesting artifacts in their hands and making the odd note. Little will be understood of modern collections-care, interpretation problems, resource management and meeting constantly improving professional standards.

People who don't work in museums include councillors, peers, MPs, local and central government officials; people with influence over the future of museums. It is very easy to overestimate how much they know about our business. We have not spent enough time explaining the role of museums. As a result when we start putting our case we often leap into what should be the middle of the conversation, instead of starting at the beginning. We need to spell out why the understanding of history is vital; what the nature of our community service is; and what sort of challenges have to be met in order to deliver these benefits.

Consider the different recent histories of libraries and museums. Their function within society is broadly the same; storage and elucidation. However, they each have very different starting points in the public's perception. For many years museums have been seen as worthy but dull, whereas we all know that books are good for you. These are simplifications, but they characterise the treatment which these two sets of similar institutions have received. There are many more splendid new library buildings than there are new museums. Also, for a decade or more museums have been under acute pressure to sharpen up, change attitudes, become more commercial, and adopt performance indicators. This pressure is only just beginning on libraries as user rates appear to be dropping. A proper comparison of functions, responsibilities and performance might have resulted in a greater degree of public investment in museums as well as libraries, but policy has not been shaped by close scrutiny and analysis; it has largely arisen from received wisdom. It is interesting to wonder whether libraries have become a statutory requirement of local authorities (whereas museums in England and Wales are not) because of this received wisdom, or through a more analytical approach. Until we can change the way people think about museums we will continue to pedal uphill.

What does this mean when it comes to lobbying at local level? Changing people's minds is a long term proposition. It needs a consistent and sustained effort for a long time. Better marketing in all its aspects will help considerably.

Just as important is the business of achieving greater contact with key opinion-formers.

Who are opinion-formers? While Ministers, Borough Treasurers, Committee Chairman might be the people to put their signatures to budget allocations, they cannot possibly research each detail of every subject on which they have to decide. They do need to be well-disposed towards you. So do local and central government officers to whom they will turn for briefing advice. These are the people who need to be supplied with all the necessary ammunition to put your case.

So, while you want the whole world to think well of you, there will always be a small number of key individuals who can really affect your future. How do you reach them? Museums usually have a good story to tell and a chance to show themselves to the best advantage. Good opinion-forming is best fostered by direct contact. Get these people into the museum as often as possible, but don't overwork them. Successive ministers have been known to leave national museums after introductory visits on their knees with fatigue, and hoping never to see another museum again. Small doses of interesting activity, together with a pocket digest of interesting facts, are much the best way to stimulate further interest. Real VIPs lead full lives, and museums are unlikely to be their main priority. In planning a visit, think carefully about one simple message you would like to get through to them, and work on how to deliver and illustrate that point.

There may be opportunities for you to meet opinion-formers at gatherings or meetings. There are meetings of local government officers at both their political and professional annual conferences, which will often have 'trade' fairs attached. Sometimes it is possible to offer a seminar or workshop – which needs to be carefully considered in terms of priorities and connections. For example, 'The future of our local museums' stands less chance of drawing an audience than 'Museums, tourism and the local economy.' Involvement with these events, whether as an observer/visitor or organiser of a stand or seminar, takes time and effort, and it is always difficult to evaluate the results. You may consider it is worthwhile if you have been able to conduct a few conversations with influential people on useful topics. The follow-up is essential, in the form of an invitation to visit for further briefing. Naturally you need to send someone to such conferences who is smart and gregarious. Shy people find it much harder to introduce themselves.

Producing a piece of print and sending it off to a mailing list of opinion-formers can be just a waste of money. Because museum people read a great deal as part of their work, it is assumed that others do too. This is not the case. Literature should be sent as an accompaniment to other direct approaches. If this has not been possible, at least send a brief personal letter introducing the literature and promising some follow-up action, either a telephone call or invitation.

All of this is labour-intensive. It is also very easy to let slip in the face of more pressing day-to-day priorities. However, for a museum which relies on public funding it is possibly the highest priority of all. Many independent museums, living in a mixed economy, would also see it as one of the most important management functions. Its not just a matter of funding either; your museum needs status within the community in order to have its views taken into account on all sorts of issues, planning in particular.

If it is seen as an important activity, but time is limited, it must obviously become part of the forward planning process. This enables a large challenge to be broken down into limited objectives over a period of time. Opinion-forming needs support from the same research activities which underpin fundraising.

PRESS RELATIONS

There are several helpful publications on this topic, so this section will confine itself to identifying key areas and exploring differences and peculiarities for museums as opposed to other types of organisations conducting press relations. There are good and bad aspects about being a museum when it comes to talking to the press. Firstly, if you are initiating the contact you are more likely than many other types of organisation to find a listening ear. Some of this is due to the greater measure of politeness accorded to a non-commercial, public benefit organisation. This is combined with a respect for expertise, which museum staff are often – but not invariably – perceived to have. In addition to these two factors is the hope that what you have to say will be 'good copy', something different, something interesting.

There is, of course, a reverse side to this coin. While offering a picture story to the local press is a fairly soft target, getting a review of an exhibition or a serious piece of work in major regionals or nationals, or on TV or radio, presents a much more difficult challenge. Art exhibitions in the national museums are firmly established as part of the circuit for reviewers. It still takes effort and communication skills to achieve appropriate levels of interest, but the channels for information-giving are established. There are art correspondents in most newspapers who, although there are over 200 art exhibitions a week in London alone, will see major museum exhibitions as part of their brief. They will be able to bring their knowledge of the subject to bear, and experience will enable them to comment upon how the exhibition is hung or otherwise presented. Now consider the position of the museum, major or minor, which wants to gain coverage for a social history, science, technological or natural history subject. There is no obvious channel of communication, because there are no correspondents who specialise in reviewing exhibitions in general. Science correspondents have to be wooed from other topics – seen as weightier topics by their editors – and, when they do visit, their experience in judging presentation skills, interpretation and educational value is meagre. The alternative, feature writers, are sometimes more accessible, but more at sea with the subject matter. Education correspondents, who should be the great allies of museums, are pre-occupied by other issues and unaccustomed to reviewing material in this form. As a result, museums are often reliant on freelance writers with an interest in the area, or 'events' coverage alongside tourist attractions and performances. Real critical judgement is lacking.

This state of affairs can be conquered. Several museums have established a good record of achievement in gaining press and media coverage with 'difficult' subject matter and from outside London. It takes consistently good press relations over a number of years to gain this kind of attention. Once you have had one good year, it is easier to maintain, foster and improve performance in this area. A co-ordinated approach under the umbrella of a marketing strategy is the only practical way forward. Just as exhibitions and events need to be geared towards target groups, so does media coverage. The appropriate channels need to be decided upon, and appropriate efforts made in those directions. For example, a transport museum might decide that train 'buffs' are finding their way to the museum in good numbers, but that family groups from just outside the immediate vicinity need to be attracted. In support of this strategy, press effort is obviously going to concentrate on local press, TV and radio in preference to the specialist magazines read by rail enthusiasts. This is an area where achievement is usually directly proportional to the amount of effort put in, so it merits conscious thought and selectivity. It is also well worthwhile in terms of cost effectiveness since, after staff costs, it comes 'free' and is regarded with far less cynicism by the reading public. Editorial coverage is about ten times as effective as advertising. Once essential guidebook entries have been paid for, money is far more effectively spent on press relations than further advertising, but the best policy of all is to have a combination of both, so that advertising reinforces editorial matter, and vice versa. Press coverage also assists profile-raising with opinion-formers and potential sponsors.

Contact lists are essential foundation work in this area. Whether you are starting from scratch or completely revising an existing list (which should be done every year), the simplest starting point is to scan newspapers and magazines, TV or Radio Times, for names of people and programmes which might be relevant to your area. Always try for a named individual, not just 'editor' or programme planner (there is one exception to this, 'picture editor' usually finds its mark without a name). There are also reference books and subscription schemes, like the PIMS or PR Planner systems. If you can network with other museums, or persuade your Area Museum Council to subscribe, there are cost savings to be made by sharing.

Timing is always important. This is where individual planning systems within a press office become essential, since every sector of press and media has different requirements. One press release on one occasion cannot meet your needs fully. Lead-in times and deadlines must be respected for purely practical reasons. Here is an example of an outline schedule for an exhibition, starting as soon as the exhibition was decided upon, two years in advance.

Two years ahead: Initial short press release and introductory letters to selected TV and radio programmes (features, not current

	affairs). During the next year this will be followed up by telephone calls, meetings and briefings.
One year ahead:	Brief press release to specialist magazines and specialist correspondents.
Six months ahead:	More detailed press release to womens' and family magazines with long deadlines. Specially written, more detailed press releases to specialist magazines and correspondents on press and media. Angle each approach to suit the specialist interest. Make second effort on TV and radio programmes.
Six weeks ahead:	Main press release to complete mailing list.
On the day:	Launch-day release, possibly with quotes from VIPs, possibly with press kit containing supplementary information. To be collected at the press view and mailed on to others.

Photographs will have been needed at the earliest possible moment, and there may be opportunities for photocalls at intervals along the way. If it is a major story, you may also telephone it through to a copy-taker at the Press Association.

Academic minds tend to over-estimate how much journalists will read, and may not be well placed to judge what will be of most interest. The author once invited the science correspondent of the Evening Standard to send her the contents of his wastepaper bin (without banana skins) for one week. The result was, among other things, 700 press releases. Whether the press read more than the first line of a press release is determined by that first line. The nub of the whole story should be in that first line or in the heading. Naturally, the more surprising, unusual, new or important you can make that story seem, the more likely it is to seem newsworthy. At the same time, you do need to keep a relationship with the truth, otherwise you will lose the trust of the journalist for future stories. That first line is your foot in the door.

Points to bear in mind:

- be brief, one side of A4
- use one-and-a-half line spacing
- use one side only of each sheet of paper
- cover *what*, *when*, *where*, *who*, but not too much *why*
- always give a contact point
- most adjectives are superfluous.

There are different kinds of press events which you may need to organise. Press views of exhibitions are the most common. Journalists like three to six weeks warning. It is important to choose a date which does not compete with other events. In London, the Arts Council of Great Britain's press office keeps a clash chart on which dates for arts and museum events can be entered and checked against one another. Mid-week is a popular time for press views. This is because Mondays are often used for office planning meetings, and some Sunday press journalists don't work on Mondays. Fridays are a bad choice because they don't allow a working day's follow-up. Light refreshments really do help a press view to go with a swing. Photographs of selected exhibits should be provided, approximately 8 x 10 inches, black and white, with clear captions and 'please return to' information on a label on the back of each. Keep a check of who comes, so that non-attenders can be sent press packs. Try to talk to as many journalists as possible and make sure they are getting interesting information or any help they may need.

Press conferences require meticulous planning. Because you have no product to show, you must have newsworthy information to give. It is a balance between giving the substance of the information in advance, and holding in reserve some remarkable quote, comment, or new piece of information. Much of the work is done on the telephone. To prevent the story being printed by one paper in advance, and consequently others losing interest, you may decide to use an embargo. This is a request not to print, publish or broadcast the information before a fixed time on a fixed day. Such a request is usually honoured, and should only be used where circumstances make it essential.

Photo-opportunities or photocalls are great tools for museum press officers. If it is possible to anticipate what will make a good picture, press photographers can be invited in, via the picture editor of the relevant papers, to photograph the event. This can be done by a telephone call, or by issuing a printed photocall – a very simple press release, headed 'photo-opportunity', giving time, place and brief description.

Examples of photocall subjects:

- major, valuable, or otherwise interesting objects being moved or placed on display
- final touches to visually interesting conservation or restoration projects
- children using a popular exhibit
- human interest events : presentations, participation events for charity, 'personality' visits
- visually curious or amusing occurrences and predicaments.

In the so-called 'silly season' in July and August, when news is slack, museums can often do well for press coverage by inviting picture editors to send a photographer along to take shots of visitors enjoying themselves. Success depends on how well the scene is described. Enthusiasm and confidence are needed to cope with most kinds of press event, and these qualities need to be balanced with a great deal of tact and good 'people' skills.

QUOTABILITY

We live in an age of 'sound bites'. Journalists of all kinds look for the quotable quote. The wise museum interviewee will recognise this and provide it. Deciding in advance what is the most newsworthy thing you have to say, and saying it in a pithy, emphatic way means that the journalist doesn't have to fish around for a quote, perhaps choosing something you feel is unhelpful.

Direct press relations, in interviews on the telephone, in person, on the radio or on TV, is all about a battle for control. You need to decide what your objective is in agreeing to be interviewed, and find a way to make your points, almost regardless of what questions are being asked. Listen to experienced politicians 'turning' a question into the one they really wanted to be asked. 'That raises some interesting points, not least of which is the issue of.....'
'What I feel that question is really getting at is.....'
'I'm glad you asked me that because it has a bearing on...'
Museum people are rarely put in real hot seats, but often feel battered by their contacts with the media. Preparation is the key. Don't just be led into an interview; discuss beforehand the ground to be covered. Most journalists will respond well to suggestions, such as, 'I have some interesting things to say about X, will I have an opportunity?' All they are trying to do is to make an interesting programme, so if you appear able to help them do that, they will let you get to the most interesting points. At the same time you must realise that an element of surprise can work in their favour – in startling an unguarded or over-stated response from you. Some thought beforehand, in conjunction with a colleague can anticipate most questions. Always have one or two examples to illustrate likely points. Most importantly, make a limited number of points, just two or maybe three. The material that you give to a journalist, in a corridor, in the lift, immediately after an interview is on the record, unless you make it clear that what you are about to say is off the record, or not attributable to you. This convention is respected.

There are all sorts of do's and don'ts connected with media appearances. The points made above are the most important, but the end results can be greatly affected by the way you sit, stand, talk or twitch. Media training with an experienced trainer is the best possible preparation, and a great deal more can be learned from it than how to look relaxed on TV. It can give insights into press techniques; how to think 'on your feet'; handling difficult situations; and how to assess newsworthiness. There are some highly readable publications on the subject in 'Helpful Books'.

RESEARCH

While the importance of visitor and non-visitor research cannot be over-stated, there are other forms of research which should underpin marketing activities. Aside from obvious fact-finding connected with direct marketing activity, such as discovering advertising rates in different media, and looking into likely effectiveness, or finding out about the existence and contents of various mailing lists, time does need to be set aside for wider forms of research to inform strategic planning, rather than specific projects. This could be said to fall into three groups:

Local knowledge
Sponsorship and development opportunities
Other people's experience.

Understanding what is going on in the wider pool from which customers are drawn is obviously vital. This means local demographics and developments. 'Local' applies to your catchment area, or intended catchment area. So a national museum, or any museum which attracts large numbers of people from a wide area, will obviously have to study national, or even international projected trends. Museums with visitors strictly from the immediate vicinity may want to look only at trends and developments from that area, or a slightly wider area. For example, the opening of the Channel Tunnel may have an important effect on museums in the South-East, or falling numbers of school-age children in a rural area will have an effect on services offered by museums in that area. All museums will feel the effects of an ageing population and of recession and post-recession prudence. This means keeping in touch with the broad view of what is going through the press and media, and by gaining access to the findings of relevant research. Local authority marketing departments can usually help in building up a picture of what is happening to local demographics, or major development projects which are planned. Tourist boards also have information on trends likely to affect tourism.

In sponsorship and development activities, information is power. Unless you can discover company objectives, you won't have much chance of aligning your projects with suitable sponsors, or of presenting a good project in a persuasive way. No research means wasted time and effort in an area which does not have a high rate of return even when well researched. Some of this can be done using publications, such as the Directory of Social Change *Guide to Company Giving*, and some will need to be done on the telephone, by asking questions. Contact-making is also a form of research, in that the more useful people you meet and talk to, the more opportunities and ideas you will get. Exactly the same applies to charitable support from trusts, and exactly the same path should be followed. Other forms of research will include keeping au fait with the broad issues of tax-effective giving, and sometimes the real nitty gritty of this subject. It can be embarrassing to win a potential donor or sponsor, only to fall at the last hurdle when questions of VAT or tax exemption arise. Keeping ears and eyes open for new grant schemes and awards is also important. Reading the professional magazines, such as Museums Journal, Museum Development, Area Museum Council newsletters, and the Association of Independent Museums Bulletin, is useful. Tapping into the grapevine among fellow museum professionals is also a good way to hear about new possibilities.

Case studies, or simply first-hand accounts of what other museums have experienced can save time and money in your own learning curve. Generally, museums are very happy to share information about their successes, and even failures, which can be just as instructive. For example, the National Gallery was among the first to experiment with late-night opening. It was a long and difficult path. Simply knowing, from the benefit of their experience, that it can take three years to establish late-night opening is a valuable piece of information. Being able to ask why and how is even better. Both the Museums & Galleries Commission and the Area Museum Councils try to encourage exchange of information through publications and forums. Sometimes there is no need to re-invent the wheel; simply adapt it.

STRATEGIC PLANNING

Marketing is a perpetual activity, so it follows that it is circular, in that action is monitored and evaluated, and this informs future definitions of objectives. Museums have been known to jump onto this cycle at any point – usually implementation – and skip the phases they feel they don't have time for. This means that learning by experience is meagre and not rationalised. Sometimes some initial research is undertaken and nothing comes of it; an equal waste of time. Each part of the cycle is dependent upon the others, and applies to long-term planning and ad hoc projects alike. See front and back sections for detailed guidance.

11. *National Museum of Wales, Cardiff.*

TARGETING

What distinguishes marketing from a low level of general publicity-seeking is targeting. After considering who is and who is not using the venue, and considering objectives, decisions can be taken as to which types or groups of people should be the subject of special efforts on the marketing front. Many museums say that they are trying to serve the widest possible spectrum of people, so their marketing effort should be aimed at a broad general public. This is the least effective way to use resources, scattering them widely over a poorly defined area. A marketing strategy will allow for different groups to be targeted in different years, so that by having limited, or clearly identified objectives, real progress can be made, measured, and built upon. It stands to reason that different types of people lead different lives and need to be reached in different ways, possibly with slightly different messages. Museums have many options here. Unlike performing arts centres, they are offering many different types of subject matter simultaneously. This is reflected in the broad social cross-section of people who use museums.

Visitor research is the obvious starting point. Once the information is assembled, decisions can be made. For example, the Pitt Rivers Museum in Oxford was concerned to maintain and increase visitor numbers on a tiny marketing budget. A visitor survey showed them that the growth they had achieved in visitor numbers was all among young and mid-career adults. This was cheering, since they could build upon this to maintain these groups into the years ahead. They also found that a typical visitor was likely to be solo, well-heeled and well-educated. They could immediately identify an opportunity to increase numbers from among local people on their doorstep, and furthermore, the survey provided strong indications of why they were not reaching more than a small proportion of that potential market. This provided options for growth. They could avoid high-cost low-return policies in favour of promising, easier to achieve objectives. They were able to see their 'general public' as being made up of different interests and perceptions, and to choose the best course of action to suit museum objectives and resources. There are always cost implications attached to target groups.

There are many different potential target groups. Here are some which could merit separate treatment and approaches:

- enthusiasts (for particular subject matter)
- clubs on group excursions
- people undertaking further education
- teachers and classes
- family groups on leisure trips.

There are many more. Even within this short list, it is evident that different reading and social habits will require approaches to be made through different media, using different language. For example, enthusiasts will read specialist magazines, special interest features in general interest magazines, and possibly newsletters from societies. This doesn't mean that they don't read and listen to all the other general news and features output that everyone else is subjected to, but you don't have to pay for, or put effort into, reaching a hundred people in the hope of catching the attention of one who is already interested in your subject matter. Likewise, you wouldn't explain what you are offering in quite the same terms to an enthusiast with a bit of knowledge of the subject as you would to a family group looking for an entertaining day out. It is said that government ministers are the most difficult group to reach, since they read nothing but briefing papers and don't have time to watch TV or listen to the radio!

It should also be evident that you can't choose target groups at whim, without reference to what you are offering. Transport and military museums sometimes seek to bridge a gap in their female attendances, or seek to attract women because of their role in deciding on and organising family days out. The first step in doing so is to look at what satisfies and interests the particular group you are trying to extend. Museums like the Bovington Tank Museum and Fleet Air Arm Museum have both extended their female audiences by discovering that the social history aspects of their collections had more appeal to most women than the history of engineering. They have adapted their approach to the presentation of some of their exhibitions accordingly. This is not always possible. However, it does put the nature of a temporary exhibition programme in a new light. Museums which decide the content and style of their programmes according to the likes and enthusiasms of their curators may be out of step with the likes and enthusiasms of visitors already attending, and a long way from widening their market.

The factors or features which have the potential to interest people are called benefits. Brainstorming groups can help to establish the benefits offered. This may result in an over-lengthy list which needs to be selectively reduced, but it can offer some new angles on the subject. Here are some of the benefits offered by a modern jewellery exhibition:

- New – first time that some of the pieces have been shown
- high standard of craftsmanship
- decorative, ornamental pieces
- many young craftspeople involved
- unusual and unconventional pieces.

Such an exhibition begins to select its own audience, consisting of younger people; those with a special interest in decorative design and craft; people interested in fashion and dress. When this is put together with potential target groups within the catchment area, it suggests art and fashion schools, clubs and classes; craft venues; specialist magazines; teenage magazines and other media. It also suggests a young, avant garde style, rather than a traditional approach.

This is a long way from standard mailing lists, one press release and a leaflet. It takes thought and imagination, but also a great deal of time and effort in order to communicate the appropriate benefits to the appropriate groups.

USING CONSULTANTS

Marketing is a continual, cyclical activity. It is an important part of the strategic planning process, and relies on performance indicators. Continuity of approach, monitoring and appraisal are requirements. This means that full-time marketing officers are needed for sustained programmes which intermesh with the management policy for the whole museum. Out of over two thousand museums in the UK, in 1992 only 40 could be identified as having marketing officers. What is the role of the consultant within this?

Consultants can provide ad hoc services to look after particular projects. They can also give informed, intelligent advice, and perhaps most importantly, a fresh view. In the museum sector, the value of this fresh view should be its understanding of the market and the practicality of the advice. The Museums & Galleries Commission has now assisted nearly one hundred museum marketing consultancies. Each one was evaluated, and some observations can be made. Firstly, small museums seem to do better with small consultancies. Larger museums often need a greater array of services – such as combined market research, corporate planning and logo design – which the big consultancies can provide as an integrated service, at a price. Secondly, some topics are a tougher challenge for short-term consultancy; in particular, merchandising advice, which is often perceived by museums as a marketing problem. Generally speaking publicity, public relations and strategic planning advice can be very successful on a short-term basis. Finally, where consultancies have proved difficult, or have failed to provide usable advice, poor briefing and unrealistic expectations seem to be the cause. A good brief and the quality and previous experience of the consultant are key factors.

To prepare a brief, focus on the specific problems you are hoping to solve. Say why you want to solve them, and start by describing the symptoms or the prevailing conditions. Too often, the solution is proposed alongside the question. For example, 'our visitor figures have reached a plateau and we want suggestions for a publicity programme to achieve an increase'. A fair question, but it inhibits the consultant from investigating other solutions. It may be that the product needs adjustment, or that local routing or competition has changed. Unless you are certain about the cause, it is more productive to describe the effects. A frequent comment by consultants is that they have been brought in to advise on a particular issue, but a different picture emerges as the consultancy develops, and the resulting advice often focuses, usually by agreement, on a different issue.

The consultant will need sufficient information on which to base advice, but not so much that an unreasonable amount of reading is required compared to the duration of the consultancy. Consultants are usually pleased to work for museums, and will be generous with their time, but there have been instances of contracts breaking down before completion due to wrong assessments of workload. Before placing a contract, and after appointment, it is wise to discuss with the consultant how the consultancy should be carried out, and how time should be apportioned. This is a way to clarify the budget, including incidental expenses, and decide the time-scale.

Don't be reluctant to state your values – the highest goals and objectives which are part of your mission. Marketing is not just about numerical achievements, it is also about quality. A good consultant will be just as happy working on how to make a free education service more effective as on how to increase revenue from a particular activity.

First and last, remind yourself, and if necessary, the consultant, that when they have departed it will be up to the museum to continue the work or to initiate a new course of action. This means, in the case of an advisory consultancy, that the advice should be suited to the resources available. Or, in the case of active consultancy service, such as running a publicity campaign, that the museum will have to cope with the aftermath. This could mean reverting to a low level of service after bolstering press and public expectations, or, at worst, patching up misunderstandings with the press.

Members of staff can feel threatened or affronted by the involvement of 'outside' consultants. Even if the service being provided is one quite beyond the capacity of the museum to deliver, the consultant may be seen as a threat. Driven by time pressures and the desire to succeed, the consultant may try to move at an uncomfortably fast pace, or make demands which seem unreasonable. It's a good idea to share with staff the reasons for seeking the consultancy and involve them in a positive way.

Weak managers sometimes use consultants as a hammer to drive home points which they feel they cannot get across themselves. This can backfire if the consultants reveal management weakness in their analysis. Weak consultants sometimes lack the courage to give the same advice to museums managers as they would to businessmen. Some of our grander institutions present a genteel and rarefied atmosphere which can overwhelm even quite grand consultancies. The higher the status of the museum, the more pleased a consultant may be to win the appointment. Critical faculties tend to waiver. 'I can't tell the British Museum *that*!' As a result, the paying client never gets told. Choose your consultant on the basis of experience and recommendation. Talk to them and see if their approach seems right for you – the right mix of tact and forthrightness perhaps. Do they readily appreciate the values of your organisation. And are they as realistic in their expectations as you are going to be in yours?

Finding consultants is getting easier. The Museums & Galleries Commission keeps a database of marketing consultants, usually recommended by Area Museum Services, but always with previous experience of working with museums, and the Arts Council of Great Britain holds one for arts marketing consultants. The National Council for Voluntary Organisations can also advise on consultants and how to conduct consultancy work. Area Museums Councils can sometimes also give advice.

When you have received the services or final report of a consultant, judge it according to whether it has fulfilled the brief and/or made practical recommendations. If there are aspects of the work with which you disagree, discuss it at the earliest opportunity. They may have good reasons for a course of action, or they may have misjudged the situation. Negotiate amendments. Decide how you are going to discuss future action with colleagues.

VALUE FOR MONEY

The Henley Forecasting Centre describes the mid 1990s as 'the prudence years'. The mood of the decade is caution. The prophetic and doomladen 'Downwave' by Robert Beckman, which in 1986 forecast the recession – indeed depression – of the '90s, speaks of prudence and caution as survival techniques, but also speaks of changing values, and predicts that 'people will have more time to enjoy what there is to enjoy. People are likely to become more alive to opportunities and ideas'. This puts museums in an interesting position of great potential and great competition. The public will become increasingly discriminating, which will make museum *content* more attractive. But museum *presentation* will increasingly be compared to a leisure sector which has benefitted from greater capital investment in past years. Museums which do not offer high standards of public facility and customer-care will become increasingly unattractive.

Quality of service delivers perceived value for money – whether we are talking about paying customers, central government and council tax payers, or overseas visitors who have decided to spend their time in one place rather than another. Value for money is something which all museums have to be seen to provide, whether they charge admission or not.

Upon entering a museum, the visitor will expect to feel comfortable and relaxed. The way to achieve this is to provide facilities and create an atmosphere which are at least the equal of other leisure and entertainment venues. Well designed, clean lavatories, cafeterias and shops, and polite staff are just the visible signs of good customer-care. To be successful and sustained, quality of service needs to enter the bloodstream of the museum. Every museum in the country should have no difficulty in abiding by the Tourist Board's National Code of Practice for Visitor Attractions. Any museum which wants to flourish through this difficult decade needs to go further. The Museums & Galleries Commission gives guidance in its 'Quality of Service in Museums & Galleries' guidelines. The National Audit Office, in its 1993 report on quality of service in five of the national museums, gives some suggested performance indicators.

The principles which underlie the MGC's guidelines in this area are that museums should make themselves publicly accountable for their standards of collections-care:

- they should promote public understanding of their collections
- they should have and implement customer-care policies which are addressed to the needs of the customer
- better access, in every sense of the word, should be provided
- museum staff should be trained in relevant aspects of public service
- constant review of customer-care needs should take place
- safety regulations should be complied with.

This list is fundamental to the nature and existence of a museum. Quality of service is not an 'extra' tacked onto curatorial activity, but an essential ingredient of management and planning.

WRITING SKILLS

Writing skills need to be suited to the purpose in hand. This means that competence in preparing learned publications does not indicate competence in writing press releases or public information literature – perhaps the reverse. Copywriting in support of marketing is not just aimed at communicating; it aims to prompt the reader to take action.

Focusing on the intended reader is the first task of the copywriter. Benefits will need to be presented in a strong, uncomplicated way. Often, museums dilute the effectiveness of their literature by trying to reflect every aspect of their museum in one fell swoop. You may have a rich diversity of all sorts of things, but you don't have to be all things to all men at the same time. Whether devising a pictorial or written presentation, you need to find the common benefit to all the groups and interests you are addressing. People read far less than we think they do. Keep it simple.

When drafting public information literature, obtain the reader's attention and provide motivation, then give essential access information clearly, including times of opening, charges, and how to get there.

The style you use will need to be appropriate to the intended target market, but needs to be phrased in the active tense: 'visit the X museum,' not 'visits may be made....'. Also, make it personal: 'enjoy a good family day out' not 'visitors can have a good family day out'. Use short sentences. A length of eight words is accessible to 95% of the reading population. Seventeen words remain accessible to 75%, but if the sentence gets as long as twenty-seven words, only 4% will be able to follow your meaning. Similarly, short paragraphs are better, and look easier to read. Clear design and layout will help. (Beware designers who try to convince you that printing the text sideways or at an angle is trendy, or that faded or tinted text will look good; this may cut out readers with impaired sight and makes it difficult for others).

Words like 'fun', 'tremendous' and 'unique' really must be backed up by substantiation. Usually it is advisable to make the substance the message. 'The world's only working weaving mill still powered by water' says it all. Additional words should be used to describe the experience in order to make it sound pleasurable as well as remarkable. When looking for headings, or key phrases to be printed typographically, use puns to appeal to your readers and alliteration to emphasise the message. 'Woven by water' used at Styal Mill, is right for the market shared with the National Trust, and has a lyrical quality which enhances the message. Grab people's attention, amplify your message, add persuasion, and make it easy to take the required action.

Word processors are of tremendous use in copywriting for marketing. Not only can you draft, change and print, but you can personalise direct mail or standard letters of approach to the press or others. The mailmerge facility helps to reduce the intense amount of labour involved in marketing.

X FACTOR

Marketing is a rational process. It follows a logical sequence of information-gathering, analysis, selection, planning, implementation, monitoring and evaluation. An additional element to do with inspiration, the creative leap, or, for the purposes of this book, the X Factor, is what singles out a sparkling campaign from a workmanlike one. The bright little idea does not always appear to order, not even as a result of meticulous analysis and logical thought. Whether the idea needed is for an exhibition title, a slogan, an image, a theme, a connection, or a perfectly matched sponsor, the rational thought process sometimes needs a little help. The term 'brainstorming' is an almost over-familiar one. It is a useful technique with positive applications, and without it 'creative' industries, like advertising, would be lost. It can play a part in a formal planning process.

A group of lively minds, not all of one 'type', with representation from, or affinity with, the target group/s, should be gathered together and confronted with the problem. A time limit should be set. Background briefing should be given, and an explanation that there is no right or wrong answer. The occasion is one for exploring possibilities, connections and associations. Everyone should be encouraged to participate. Silly ideas should be noted alongside sensible ones, so that after the meeting the results can be considered and useful material extracted.

In any organisation, there is usually a sharp-witted person who wins the caption competitions and offers the pithy comment on events. They may be just the person to come up with a good title. Keeping in touch with the market is also important. The Natural History Museum hesitated for two years before christening their insect exhibition 'Creepy-Crawlies'. At planning stage it seemed to denigrate the expert advice which was being concentrated on the content. In the event, it was a winning title which immediately conveyed what it was about, and sounded exciting and accessible to the intended audience.

Obscure titles can be made to work, but only if the publicity support is sufficient to make them familiar.

'Yoruba' at the Horniman needed serious marketing commitment to generate the interest aroused. The title 'Pompeii' was a gift, not just because people immediately understood the subject being offered, but because the word is emotionally 'loaded'. Sir Roy Strong's comment that 'either death, sex, or jewels are vital ingredients for a blockbuster' has more than a grain of truth in it. Alliteration can help too. 'Mighty Mammoth' was a strong title. Short, evocative titles are effective because they are more memorable, make more impact, and are more likely to look good on printed material.

So inspiration and creativity are important and, if they don't occur naturally, a collective approach can help to solve the problem. Perhaps the greatest skill is in recognising the X-Factor when it arises.

YIELD

Pricing is an aspect of marketing which involves a great deal of time and trouble in the commercial sector. Museums pay inadequate attention to it. Finding the right level to charge for goods or services is difficult because we don't have the usual baselines from which to operate. Nearly all museums receive some level of public subsidy, so establishing a cost price can be tricky. If the V&A were to charge admission at cost price, it would be well over £10 per visitor. Many catalogues and publications would be beyond the reach of most visitors, and many services which are now modestly priced would price themselves out of the market. Awareness of this leads museums into a pricing trap. In having to 'invent' a price, figures seem to be plucked out of the air.

Comparison, through even the simplest levels of research, is the way to arrive at a proper price. What is being charged for comparable goods and

12. Children from a local school in 1880's costume for a photocall at the Natural History Museum's 100th birthday.

services to similar target groups? When looking at admission charges, find out what people are paying for cinema seats and visits to local theme parks or other leisure attractions. How does your museum compare in terms of pleasure, interest and length of visit? Many directors worry about making charges too high, and say they want to lag behind the market, rather than to lead it. The implications of delaying a price increase are rarely properly charted. A museum can easily get into a position of constantly being behind what the market will bear. This can act on finances in a rather similar way to compound interest, to the detriment of the museum. A simplification of pricing policy on admissions is to keep on a par with other attractions; if in doubt, err on the high side, but offer generous discounts and free periods during quiet times. 'Concessions' are used, for reasons of social conscience, to make the museum accessible to students, the unemployed, or to local residents. 'Discounts' are a marketing tool to shape business in an appropriate way: to encourage repeat visits or to encourage more visitors in groups, or to incentivise membership of schemes which benefit the museum. In practice concessions and discounts are the same thing, but their function and effect are different.

Concessions on admission prices are part of your incentive structure as well as a socially-conscious offer which helps to fulfil the mission statement. They need to be seen as part of the calculated pricing structure for two reasons. Demographic changes, or sudden increases in the numbers of a particular group, can affect forward planning calculations. Also, when targeted at group travel, such as senior citizens' excursions, they become a direct selling tool. (Incidentally you must not discriminate on an age/sex basis, offering cheaper admission to a woman of 60 than a man of 60. Call it 'senior citizens' and interpret it generously).

Low prices do not mean increased attendances. Perceived value has a lot to do with this. There is a common assumption that something which is cheap is of lower quality than something which is not. But prices do need to be kept within people's capacity to pay.

In the forward planning process, an estimate of yield from a number of different sources needs to be calculated. Averaging out expenditure per visitor provides a yield figure which can be used as a performance indicator and to assist targeting. Many museums make calculations of spend per head in museum shops. This is a useful indicator, but does not tell the whole story. Pricing in museum shops is often erratic. Some museums arrive at prices by adding the same mark-up to each item sold. This is a poor way to arrive at a price, and usually results in underpricing, although it can lead to overpricing. There can even be inconsistency of pricing within different shops in the same museum service, where different standard mark- ups have been used. There is a 'right' retail price for any item, to do with what people are prepared to pay, and it has nothing to do with standard mark-up.

Museum catering outlets have a captive market. Visitors really do need to pause and take refreshment during their visit, so it is tempting to charge high prices. Unless you are providing truly pleasant surroundings with good quality, well presented food and drink, people will resent high prices, resulting in dissatisfied customers. Only high standards justify high prices.

Museums often offer other services for which they make a charge. New services are easier to price than long established ones. A museum entering the corporate hospitality market will be able to assess costs from the outset, the only difficult part being the premium charged for the use of exclusive surroundings. Setting charges high, with room to negotiate downwards, is a reasonable approach, but don't be afraid to negotiate upwards if extra services and difficulties are involved. The same applies to facility fees for film and photography, a generally under-priced area of museum activity.

ZAP LISTS

A possible difference between a good marketing officer and a good academic is the speed at which they can work. Both rely on tried and tested disciplines but, due to time pressures, the marketing officer often has to put these into practice very swiftly. Even working within a carefully planned, time-pointed strategy, the marketing officer, as the interface with the outside world, often has to respond instantaneously to unanticipated events or requirements. In these circumstances, the challenge is to meet the deadline in the most appropriate way. The academic must put academic integrity first, even if it means missing a deadline. A better understanding of the different priorities at work should lead to more harmonious relations and an ability to help one another.

13. *A survey of this queue at the V&A for the first* Fabergé *exhibition showed motivation in response to 'advertisements' when nothing but editorials had appeared.*

As an aid to anyone working under pressure, whether marketing officer or curator acting as marketing officer, a few readily accessible lists can save a lot of time and trouble. There are three lists which should always be on hand at the office and at home. Their existence will mean that, with the aid of a telephone, and possibly a fax machine, more can be accomplished swiftly and effectively than starting from scratch.

Emergency List: as covered in the section on planning for emergencies, the marketing or press officer should have a place on the 'call-out tree', so that when notified they can spring into pre-arranged action using a list with vital telephone numbers to contact media and inside and outside advisers, plus the handy phrases which assist accurate reporting under pressure.

Hot List: a list of key media names, telephone and fax numbers, starting with the Press Association, for use in the event of sudden important happenings, such as a swift financial or political blow to the organisation, a need to raise money or obtain action on behalf of a threatened object, or some sudden benefaction. This list can also be used to chase up attendances at press conferences.

Photo List: a list of picture editors' and photo-agencies' telephone and fax numbers in order to put out a quick photocall. There are occasions when opportunities arise suddenly – a celebrity walks through the doors; a large exhibit being delivered gets stuck in a doorway; an enormous queue forms for a new exhibition; or a public event proves particularly popular and photogenic. The opportunist needs be prepared. Along with press numbers it may be wise to have your security chief's number or extension, in order to advise of what's going on, or request assistance.

If there is a press officer in addition to the marketing officer, he or she should hold these lists, but remember, everyone takes a holiday at some point, so deputies are needed and everyone needs to be clear about who is the duty officer. Most importantly, lists go out of date quickly. Regular updates are needed.

In calmer moments checklists can help to ensure that nothing has been forgotten, either in planning or implementation.

Planning Checklist

- Are the overall and specific objectives clearly stated?
- Has the target market been identified?
- Have the ways of reaching the target market been explored?
- Have these ways been costed?
- Have decisions been made about ways and means in relation to resources available?

- Is there a time-pointed plan for the campaign or strategy?
- What are the plans to monitor effectiveness?
- How can the resulting evaluation help future work?

CASE STUDIES

A SHORT-TERM MUSEUM MARKETING CONSULTANCY

Under a scheme administered by the Museums & Galleries Commission, a number of grants were issued each year to assist with short-term consultancies.

This was a one day consultancy carried out by the Ylva French Consultancy. The museum regarded the brief as having been fulfilled completely, with added bonuses. Many of the recommendations have been adopted.

CANTERBURY HERITAGE MUSEUM

Marketing Report and Recommendations

1. Objectives

The objectives of the one-day consultancy were to evaluate the identity of the Canterbury Heritage Museum, make recommendations on how it could raise its profile and achieve increased attendances through an active marketing campaign within the restrictions of the budget.

2. Canterbury and its Attractions

a. Canterbury attracts an estimated one million visitors a year, half of whom are staying visitors. Canterbury is the 14th most popular destination within England for overseas visitors, and attracts an estimated 150,000 staying visitors a year from overseas (source: Canterbury Tourism Survey, 1985). In addition the town has a population of 30,000 and the surrounding area more than double that.

b. The main attraction is the Cathedral which receives an estimated 2.25m visits a year. In the last two years, Canterbury has seen the establishment of two new attractions, the Canterbury Heritage Museum operated by Canterbury City Council, opened in 1987, and Pilgrim's Way, operated by Heritage Projects Ltd., opened a year later.

c. Canterbury Heritage Museum is located in Stour Street, slightly away from the centre of the town, whereas Pilgrim's Way is next to the Visitor Information Centre in the heart of the town. The latter has enjoyed higher visitor figures, and yet it has apparently not met its target. It is being re-launched in May as Pilgrim's Trail.

d. Canterbury Council appears to have downgraded the importance of tourism, privatised the tourist information centre, and put other initiatives such as a new coach park on hold. A sign-posting scheme is being introduced but has not been completed.

e. The Cathedral has recently appointed a new visitor services manager and is committed to 'visitor management', which includes encouraging visitors to see other parts of Canterbury to take the pressure off the Cathedral.

f. According to the South East England Tourist Board, Canterbury suffers from its high flow of day visitors which has produced a 'candy-floss' image, surprising for a Cathedral town. There is a large number of young French and English school groups whose very presence is a discouragement to other, more serious visitors.

g. The latest addition to the town, Guide Friday, is a sightseeing and tour operating company, established in Stratford on Avon, Cambridge, Windsor and other centres. Their presence will help to generate a flow of independent visitors round the town by open-topped bus, and in the longer run they may promote packages into Canterbury.

3. The Image of the Canterbury Heritage Museum

a. Without in depth research, it is only possible to give a subjective view of the image of the Canterbury Heritage Museum, based on conversations and impressions.

b. Within the tourist industry Canterbury Heritage Museum is seen as an imaginative attraction which has been supported by an ETB grant, and awarded a Come to Britain commendation.

c. Visitors, once inside, appreciate the attractive building and informative displays, but may be confused not only by the appearance of the building, but also the name and printed material. The historic building does not immediately appear to be a museum, and better signing is suggested, see below.

d. The logo-style and wording chosen for the museum's printed material conveys a slightly confused message – something between a heritage centre, a themed attraction and possibly a museum. This is no doubt the result of some confusion as to the true objectives of the museum, established when the vogue was for 'heritage centres' and 'themed attractions', and Pilgrims' Way was due to open.

e. Canterbury Heritage Museum has a unique and distinct role to fulfil as the historical museum of Canterbury, telling the history of one of the most important towns in England, and acting as the repository of treasures of the town's past, still being uncovered. Its audiences are three-fold: the people of Canterbury and Kent, visitors from other parts of England, and visitors from overseas. It is not 'a place of entertainment' or 'a themed attraction'. It is very much a museum of its time, using the best of the imaginative display techniques now available, with space to grow and develop.

Recommendation 1

Canterbury Heritage Museum should restate its objectives as the Museum of Canterbury's 2,000 year-long history. It has a unique role and status in the town, and should distinguish itself very clearly from places of entertainment, such as Pilgrim's Trail. Its primary objective must be to attract those visitors which have an interest in Canterbury's history, and those who would enjoy learning more.

Recommendation 2

In view of the shortage of funds, a complete rethink on the logo and house-style is not suggested at this point. However, in preparation for the completion of the second phase of the museum, and the re-opening of the Roman house, also run by the Museum department, a new corporate identity for all the museums is suggested. Preparation for this should start in 18 months time.

4. NUMBER OF VISITORS TO CANTERBURY HERITAGE MUSEUM

a. The visitor figures provided show a decline from 43,000 in financial year 1989 to 39,000 in 1990. This is partly due to the hot summer which affected a number of visitor attractions; the museum also benefited from a special Rupert Bear exhibition in financial year 1989.

b. It is estimated that 70 per cent of visitors are adults, 30 per cent are children; only recently has differential pricing allowed for a distinction between children and old age pensioners. This already shows a high percentage of OAPs. Approximately 17 per cent of visitors came in a group. An estimated 40 per cent came from overseas.

c. The length of visit is estimated at 40 to 60 minutes and the maximum capacity at any one time, 200. The peak day is Saturday; but the museum is open only half the day on Sundays in summer. Peak months based on previous years are August and October (special exhibition) with March, April, May, June, July and September showing a similar figure of between 3,000 and 4,000 a month.

d. The price charged is £1.20 for adults, 90p for OAPs, and 60p for children. This will not change in 1990. Some visitors have been observed turning away when informed of the charge.

Recommendation 3

In order to have access to visitor figures, clearly broken down on a monthly basis, it is suggested that a computerised till and program are installed. This should indicate adult, child, and OAPs, time of day, day, domestic or overseas (if possible), groups.

Recommendation 4

To back this up and to provide information for future planning, a visitor research programme is suggested. A standard questionnaire from AMSSEE is enclosed which could be adapted by the museum and self-administered. Consideration should be given to qualitative research which could encompass the three museums. This could possibly be undertaken in conjunction with one of the educational institutions in the town to save on costs.

Recommendation 5

The price of admission is about right in relation to length of visit. No immediate price increases are suggested.

5. SIGNPOSTING

a. The black and gold sign-posting which has been partly introduced in the town is designed to be unobtrusive to the point of being unnoticeable and difficult to read. With perseverance they can be followed from the Cathedral to the museum, and with gaps from the Canterbury East Station to the museum.

b. Free-standing maps exist with commercial advertisements but only one was observed outside the station.

Recommendation 6

Canterbury Council should be encouraged to replace the gold on the black sign-posting with white, so that it is more legible. The sign-posting should be completed so that it covers the whole town without noticeable gaps.

Recommendation 7

Additional free-standing maps with (appropriate commercial advertising) should be erected. The exits from the Cathedral are important *decision points* 'Where do I go from here?'. These are the ideal spots to encourage a wider distribution of visitors throughout Canterbury.

6. FACILITIES AND FUTURE PLANS

a. The Museum is on two floors in a medieval building backing on to the River Stour. Two adjoining buildings have been acquired and will be incorporated into the museum of the next two years. There are nine separate areas, some very spacious. As the building does not look like a museum and is located off the beaten track, signing on the building is important. This is restricted by the historic nature of the building to freestanding posters along the entrance.

Recommendation 8

An additional sign to be erected on the flint wall facing Bear Cart Lane. If possible an additional sign to be erected on the building (not of historic interest) facing Hawks Lane. It should be possible to identify these signs from a distance.

b. The Museum currently has no public lavatories and no cafeteria. An informal survey carried out has shown the former to be a major requirement by visitors, and staff are allowed to let visitors use the private staff lavatories. Both these facilities are planned for the second phase.

Recommendation 9

It is clear that the absence of lavatories is a source of irritation and has a detrimental effect on 'word of mouth' recommendation. *Priority* should be given to the immediate installation of lavatory facilities, even on a temporary basis, pending the redevelopment of the adjoining buildings.

Recommendation 10

Consideration should be given to the size and style of cafeteria to be provided in the second phase. Experience elsewhere show that for museums of any size, an imaginatively run cafeteria (independently catered) can be an important additional attraction to the museum, and a source of income.

c. The shop area is at present limited and so is the content. The person who operates the till is also responsible for this, and any enlargement of the shop would have to take this into consideration. Plans for a separate shop form part of the second phase. Items on sale include postcards, booklets and some Cafeteria Bear memorabilia.

Recommendation 11

In order to increase income, it is suggested that new products unique to the Canterbury Heritage Museum, are developed, which can be sold within the existing, improved display. This could include a postcard of the building, replicas of some of the items in the museum, e.g. the pilgrims' badges, a cut-out modelling kit of Roman Canterbury etc. This means that a wider range of products for sale will be available when the shop opens.

d. At present functions are welcome at the museum if they have a direct connection with the museum. They are seen as a form of goodwill and no charge (except for catering) is made. Roughly 10 a year take place for up to 200 people.
The attractive Great Hall and other spacious rooms make this potentially a sought-after venue for which a commercial rate could be charged. The need to have curatorial staff present at such functions in addition to security charge, however, puts pressure on limited staff resources.
Plans for the adjoining building include an education centre which would be available to the University of Kent and other out of town educational institutions.

Recommendation 12

It is suggested that a separate investigation is made into the commercial possibility of the museum as a hospitality venue, taking into account the plans for future expansion, including the cafeteria and education centre. This should look particularly at any additional staffing requirements in relation to existing staff resources, not just to operate the facilities but also to market them, in relation to the potential commercial income.

e. There is no car parking at the museum but this is a Canterbury wide problem and therefore does not impact directly on the museum. A new coach park is planned across the River near the museum with a footbridge which would take visitors passed the museum. This would obviously be a major asset for the museum, as well as the town as a whole.

Recommendation 13

The Council should be encouraged to progress the coach park in the interest of all the attractions in Canterbury and to take the opportunity in the coach park to provide information in clear pictorial form to encourage visitors to disperse through the town.

f. Special exhibitions planned for the future include a Cafeteria Bear exhibition in November to coincide with the Canterbury Festival. The museum has already held such an exhibition which attracted considerable interest.

Recommendation 14

Contact should be made with Express Newspapers Publicity Department (Ian Walker) to discuss promotion of the exhibition and possible financial support from Express Newspapers for a permanent Cafeteria Bear exhibition in second phase.

7. MARKETING AND PUBLICITY

a. Current marketing and public relations activities include distribution of A5 leaflet in three languages, a joint Canterbury leaflet, participation in trade affairs and exhibitions, liaison with other attractions in Canterbury including guest houses, regular contact with local newspapers and radio and ad hoc mailing of press releases.

b. Current print includes the A5 leaflet in English, French and German and the joint educational leaflet; stock is now low of all of these. 100,000 were produced of the English A5 leaflet, and 15,000 of French and German. The German language leaflet has not been in high demand.

c. Distribution is handled mainly by the marketing officer and includes mailing to new leads. Piggy-backing on the Marlow Theatre distribution system free of charge will no longer be possible. A central leaflet distribution system for guest houses is being organised.

Recommendation 15

It would be cost-effective for Canterbury Heritage Museum to employ a leaflet distribution company. This would allow the marketing officer to use her time more productively.

Recommendation 16

The current general leaflet should be replaced by a 1/3 of A4 leaflet in full colour, using some of the very good colour transparencies already available, plus one of the

outside of the building. If the budget allows, a separate French language leaflet in the same style should be produced at the same time, but not German.

Recommendation 17

To set in motion a new joint Canterbury on View leaflet, based on the successful educational leaflet. The arrival of Guide Friday may provide the impetus for this, as well as the change of name of Pilgrims' Way.

d. The Museum has no guide-book or teachers' packs of information sheets. Informal research has shown that both of these are in demand. In order to raise its profile as a museum as opposed to 'a themed attraction', it is essential that the museum develops a guide for sale with colour illustrations but also detailed coverage of the exhibition and a feature on Canterbury's history, perhaps in date form. Teacher's fact sheets can be free in small quantities but saleable for larger numbers. Both these will generate income.

Recommendation 18

That a guide to the museum is put in hand without delay, target price £1 or £1.25; and alongside this, teacher's fact sheets are developed available separately or as a pack.

e. The museum has been able to participate in trade fairs at a very low cost and it is suggested that this programme is continued with the possible addition of Moot in May 1991, if it goes ahead. The impact will be greater if the museum participates jointly with other 'Canterbury on View' attractions.

Recommendation 19

To participate in trade fairs possibly including Moot in May 1991, as part of 'Canterbury on View'.

f. Very little advertising is undertaken. Without a larger budget it is suggested that this policy is continued, and advertising limited to local guides.

g. Since its opening the museum has not actively encouraged the London-based travel and tourist boards to visit the museum. Occasional press visitors have come through SEETB and Pilgrim's Way.

Recommendation 20

Canterbury Heritage Museum to organise a series of familiarisation visits in the autumn for the travel trade, tour operators, travel writers and tourist boards, as a joint enterprise with other Canterbury attractions.

h. Good contacts are now established with Boulogne and Calais. No direct contact has been established with BTA Paris.

Recommendation 21

That the marketing officer visits BTA Paris to establish contact and obtain advice and information on tours and operators with a possible interest in the museum and Canterbury.

i.   It is important to maintain contact with travel editors and travel writers who may be planning features on Canterbury or the South East of England. Regular mailings are important.

Recommendation 22

That a press release about the museum and the new exhibition is sent out with the new leaflet when available, to travel writers and travel editors, generally.

j.   During the winter a special admission charge will be available for Canterbury Residents. It will be important to publicise this and to encourage repeat visitors. Public relations activities will be particularly important.

Recommendation 23

To publicise the special admission charge to 'Canterbury's own museum' with cooperation from local newspapers and local radio just before the launch, and then to repeat this early in the New Year, with a news angle – perhaps on the number of people who have already taken advantage of the reductions.

MUSEUMS ALIVE!

MUSEUMS MARKETING TOGETHER IN YORKSHIRE & HUMBERSIDE

The Yorkshire and Humberside region has about 200 museums, small and large, and the Area Museum Council wanted to initiate a sustainable project which would achieve profile for the museums, raise marketing awareness and standards, and encourage museums to work together where appropriate. The following is an abbreviated account of a project financially supported by MGC, which not only met immediate objectives, but continues, four years later, in the form of joint promotional literature.

The aims of the project were to increase the public and media awareness of museums in the area and to raise consciousness of the achievements of the profession and to bring attention to the widening appeal of museums. Also, to elucidate the importance of the collections held, the importance of museums within the economic structure of the region – in terms of tourism, education and social values. And, last but not least, to increase the number of visitors attending museums and art galleries within the region.

It was to act as a parallel promotion to the 1989 'Museums Year' campaign run by the Museums Association. As it was regional and national in scope, it was intended to amplify the voice of Museums Year rather than mute it through duplication.

The objectives of the project were:

- To hold basic training workshops in marketing for the region's professional and voluntary curators.

- To produce a series of publications highlighting co-ordinated events taking place in the region's museums in 1989.

- To provide regular information to national, regional and local press, radio and television.

- To promote six marketing seminars for curators, using outside consultants.

- To carry out marketing case studies of six selected museums in the region. These are to be carried out by consultants who will then produce a marketing plan.

MUSEUMS ALIVE! PHASE I

Promotional literature and training

The name of the campaign, Museums Alive! was decided upon in June 1988. It was intended to be lively, alluding to the fact that museums are primarily active places for people to go to, rather than assemblages of objects appealing to the learned few. A consultant was appointed as the project co-ordinator with wide-ranging experience across the arts and heritage field.

The booklet

The first priority was to produce a publication giving limited details of the regions museums. A designer was contracted on a freelance basis to produce designs and layout for the publications. He was chosen for his originality and experience of working in museums, interpretation and publishing. Project stationery was printed.

The booklet had initially been planned as a 2 colour folded flier, to be ready for the World Travel Market in December 1988. By August 1988 this had changed. The consultant had approached the Yorkshire & Humberside Tourist Board and the English Tourist Board with a view to producing a larger booklet for the region in A5 format. YHTB contributed £1,000 and ETB £2,500. The estimated production cost was £8,500 for 50,000 copies. Museums Alive! provided the design and retained editorial control.

The advertising income needed to generate the required production cost raised some interesting, if rather disappointing conclusions. The consultant had hoped that each museum could pay a fixed rate of £33.00 for their entry in the booklet.

Dialogue between the YHMC and curators revealed that many museums, especially in the local authority sector, did not have budget heads for publicity and could not release even this small amount of money. For some small independents it was a lot of money.

Instead larger advertising space was offered to those who could afford it, and smaller entries were subsidised by the project.

The time scale for production was very tight as the project had expanded. Greater detail was needed for the booklet which included a brief description of each museum, its full address and telephone number, plus a guide to car parking, restaurant, toilet and disabled facilities. Nevertheless, it was produced well in time for distribution at the World Travel Market, and through other organs such as Tourist Information Centres, Museums etc. The bulk of the booklets went to non-museums in order to attract people who were not regular museum users. A copy of the distribution list was sent to MGC. The distribution was to the Yorkshire and Humberside Region and the large urban areas on its fringes; Manchester, Liverpool, Nottingham, Derby, Newcastle and Tyneside. North Sea Ferries were also used as a distributor because of their dual role in reaching people travelling through the region and foreign tourists entering into it.

Monitoring the impact of the booklet was important. It was decided to introduce a competition, encouraging people to go out and visit six museums, which would then entitle them to enter a competition. Each museum in the booklet was issued with a rubber stamp bearing a unique number. The competitor's guide could be stamped at the museum and when the forms are returned (closing date 30 November 1989) we will be able to see which museums were visited. Competitors also have to complete a slogan stating which museum they believed to be the most alive. This will give us qualitative as well as quantitative information. The booklet also included a coupon inviting people to be placed on a mailing list for the three Events Brochures of 1989.

Marketing workshops

In addition to the booklet, Museums Alive! held four regional workshops. The purpose was twofold, to introduce the project and to introduce the basic concepts of marketing. These proved a useful way of introducing the project, augmenting what had been placed in the YHMC members mailing. The consultant's notes were available to all delegates at the workshops. It was noticeable that the greatest cynicism for the project came from within the Local Authority sector at the Leeds meeting. Most went away happier than they had arrived.

The leaflet campaign – a festival of museums

Three seasonal leaflets, highlighting events at museums were planned for 1989. As soon as the main booklet was completed the consultant began compiling information, based on the 1989 Centenary data-base prepared by YHMC listing Museums Year activity in the region.

The themes of these Spring, Summer and Autumn leaflets were:

- New Developments and Regional Personalities plus Diary of Events.

- Industrial and Craft Skills of the region plus Diary of Events.

- Museums open for business in the off peak Tourist Season plus Diary of Events.

All of these had a print run of 70,000 and were designed in a style that related to the booklet. They were all produced on time and promoted on regional 'festival' of museum activities which could be enjoyed by the public. All were distributed following the pattern established by the booklet. Copies of all three were sent to MGC. The third leaflet was presented to all delegates at the Museums Association Centenary Conference in York in September 1989.

Training

A key component of the project was to increase awareness of marketing amongst museum curators and to provide further training for them. In such a way this initiative would have a longer life than its initial twelve months.

The Marketing Workshops were important introductions to an audience that had a healthy cynicism of marketing as an overlay on their already large body of work which had to be executed within limited often inadequate resources. A marketing course was held, consisting of 6 one-day sessions over a period of 6 weeks. This was tutored by an additional outside consultant, and attracted middle managers from all over the region.

The majority of the participants were at Keeper or Assistant Keeper level. At first sight it would appear that they had little responsibility for marketing but it became clear that curators of smaller museums certainly did have to carry out this work. Also, individual Keepers in larger services had to carry out marketing and publicity work for their own projects. The course involved a great deal of practical work and was well received by all the delegates.

YHMC carried out an evaluation of the course and those participants who responded felt that it was relevant and useful to them in their current posts.

It was noted that the number of senior professionals was low. Only five of the participants were in senior management posts. YHMC feels that this could be a future target area for training within the region, especially since the appointment of a Training Officer in January 1990. Sadly there was no one from the Independent sector. This was largely due to the fact that the sessions were held midweek and that this was difficult for volunteers with weekday commitments.

14. *Geffrye Museum, London.*

MUSEUMS ALIVE! PHASE II

Consultancies & incentive funding

The second phase of the project was designed to give real, practical help to member museums in the Yorkshire and Humberside Region. The booklet and leaflet campaigns had already proved to be a success and were welcomed by the profession, who now saw that 'marketing' was something that they were involved in and could control on their own terms.

Implementation

It was agreed that the consultant used in Phase I would continue to work with a number of museums, galleries and services to help those bodies create a two year marketing plan.

The overall objectives of the plan were:

- to create a two year marketing plan for each individual museum, gallery or service

- to enable the individual museums to make the best of the present resources and to positively market those resources to the general public.

- to help them begin to develop an overall 3 year business plan alongside the marketing plan

- to offer practical assistance to each individual museum to enable them to apply to YHMC for the Incentive Funding Monies attached to Museums Alive!

- to ensure that all these initiatives were suitably monitored.

Six consultancies were to be offered, and notice was given in the May issue of YHMC members mailing. Members were invited to respond with a brief statement by 30 June 1989.

Selected schemes

The following services were selected to receive approximately £1,500 worth of consultancy time (plus expenses) and a cash grant of approximately £1,100 to commence marketing activity. All the following agreed to match this by a further £1,100 except Malton who contributed £250.

1. Large Local Authority – Hull Museums & Art Gallery

It was felt that there would be only sufficient consultancy time to tackle one large local authority service and Hull has invested considerable resources in creating new museums for transport, archaeology and social history. However, despite these developments they have spent relatively little on any form of marketing and would welcome further assistance. As part of the consultancy it is hoped to establish the need for Hull to appoint their own marketing officer for what is a very large service with obvious retailing and other income generating opportunities.

2. Small Local Authority

a. Baysgarth Museum, Glanford Borough Council

Baysgarth Museum has had considerable investment in the last few years from Glandford Council, YHMC, the Yorkshire & Humberside Tourist Board and latterly the MGC Capital Fund. Its permanent displays are now of good quality but the museum (which is set in an attractive park) does not achieve anything like the visitor numbers that it should. This year's trends, as a result of the Museums Alive! promotion, have been very encouraging and it is hoped that visitor numbers will increase quite substantially with the advice of a marketing consultant. The Glandford Leisure Officer is keen to support the marketing strategy and take it to the local authority for further support if necessary.

b. Hawes Museum, North Yorkshire County Council

The Upper Dales Folk Museum at Hawes is administered by the Yorkshire Museum in York. It is currently undergoing extensive refurbishment and the new extension will treble its size by next summer. The site itself will link with Yorkshire Dales National Park Centre and presents a major marketing opportunity. The museum is in a very remote town which has a highly seasonal visitor pattern.

3. Rural Independent – The North Holderness Museum of Village Life, Hornsea.

Hornsea Museum won the Small Museum of the Year Award in 1980 and its numbers peaked in the following year. Since then there has been a gradual decline in visitor numbers although they have picked up within the current year. In marketing terms we were confident that it would be possible to attract a greater number of visitors to reach the 1981 levels. Although Hornsea is a very small seaside town it is so highly seasonal in its visitor influx that it typifies many small rural museums of folk life.

4. Urban Independent – Malton Museum

Malton museum is situated in an attractive market to the east of York. It has extremely high quality displays of archaeology relating to the Roman Fort and civilian settlement and has recently embarked on a more ambitious programme of temporary exhibitions relating to the social history of the district. Again its visitor numbers have begun to climb this year assisted by the Museums Alive campaign, but there is considerably more scope for further visitors, particularly from the education sector.

5. Co-operative Scheme – Discover Cromwell's England, lead authority Kirklees Metropolitan Council

West Yorkshire has a number of interesting houses dating from pre industrial periods which are now in public ownership as part of the various district museum services. This project attempts to link properties such as Oakwell Hall (Kirklees), Bolling Hall (Bradford), Shibden Hall (Calderdale) and others in Leeds. Part of the consultancy will involve putting a package together of appropriate properties that will link coherently. The promotion will then link the various sites and perhaps involve joint activities to reach a wider audience. Each of these houses, although broadly similar in date, is treated quite differently from the visitor interpretation point of view and should offer a geographically compact group that will be of interest to the education sector as well as the general visitor.

Evaluation of Museums Alive!

The interim report noted the key areas where the project would be evaluated, namely:

- response to the competition
- replies to the mailing list
- overall visitor figures for the region for 1989, compared with 1988.
- media coverage
- increased museum activity in marketing

These aspects require both quantitative and qualitative approaches. Within the context of the projects objectives, it must be remembered that YHMC was starting from a low threshold of awareness. Few local authority museums had earmarked marketing budgets and there was a general distrust of the term. The smaller Independent museums were quick to realise that marketing and publicity were linked. Like the Local Authority sector few of them had special marketing budgets.

The competition offered further and continued scope for local publicity, in announcing results and awarding prizes. After quantifying, it was revealed that a small proportion of those who took up the booklet entered the competition. A sample analysis of the stamps indicates that competitors visited museums local to them but also went further afield within the region, as the following examples show.

FROM CONTESTANT: MUSEUMS VISITED

Sheffield   Bishops House, Sheffield; NMPFTV,
                   Bradford; Bolling Hall, Bradford;
                   Calderdale Industrial Museum, Halifax; Tolson Museum,
                   Huddersfield; Graves Art Gallery Sheffield

Huddersfield   Calderdale Industrial Museum, Halifax; Abbey House
                   Museum, Leeds; Shibden Hall, Halifax; NMPFTV, Bradford;
                   Bankfield Museum, Halifax; Bradford Industrial Museum

Leeds   Leeds City Museum; Leeds City Art Gallery; Museum of
                   History of Education, Leeds University; Horsforth Museum;
                   Manor House Museum, Ilkley; Oakwell Hall, Kirklees.

This is encouraging. The Museums Alive! booklet and leaflets drew together very diverse groups of museums and the sampling of the competition entrants indicates that they did not always 'collect' their six museums on the doorstep.

Replies to the mailing list

The Museums Alive! booklet carried a cut out coupon for those who required to be placed on a mailing list to receive the Museums Alive! leaflets. Fifty six applications were received. Again, this was encouraging. Although it is only a small figure it indicated a core of committed museum visitors who were interested in the leaflet campaign before it began. It is noticeable that the number of enquiries from this source began to fall once the leaflets had been produced.

November–April 1989–43 responses
April–December 1989–13 responses

To this can be added the number of personal letters asking for details and a copy of the booklet which did not state where they found the address. YHMC received a total of 177 requests for the booklet.

Overall Visitor Figures for the Yorkshire and Humberside Region

At the beginning of 1989 all YHMC member museums were asked to submit their total number of visits during 1988. This exercise was to be repeated again in early 1990. Although a crude indicator, visit numbers are useful for a project such as this. Many museums only count the total number and do not have the resources to carry out visitor surveys which investigate important areas such as

- time and distance to travel to venue

- first time visitor

- age group.

Given that one aim of the project was to increase awareness and visits, total numbers were useful as it did not matter whether they included the same visitors visiting different museums. The number of visits was more important than the number of individual visitors. Before looking at the results certain factors must be borne in mind. Firstly, the 1988 figures supplied were often approximations, especially among non-charging museums. It was noticeable that more accurate figures appeared on the returns for 1989. It may have been that the fact that YHMC had asked for figures had led to better record keeping. Secondly, the remarkable long, hot and sunny summer of 1989 which influenced people to take days out of doors in the country and at the coast. Thirdly, the effects on school visits by the Education Reform Act was beginning to have an effect on some museums within the region. The effect of such a campaign must be viewed in the longer term. YHMC intends to continue monitoring the figures over the next five years to account for seasonal and meteorological variations.

Given the problems outlined above, these figures are encouraging, showing a modest rise within the region. They are an indicator of the popularity of museums and fulfil the third stated aim of Museums Alive!

Media coverage

The majority of the media contact was carried out by the consultant with full consultation with the YHMC Director and Assistant Director (Curatorial) who maintained editorial control. A series of themed press releases was issued throughout the year. Resulting coverage and enquiries were monitored and reported upon. Extensive coverage in printed media, both general and specialised and TV and radio features were achieved. (Full listing available in separate report.) This aspect of the project was generally acknowledged to have been successful, and monitored responses are a testimony to the effectiveness.

Increased museum activity in marketing

This is a more difficult area to evaluate. An encouraging indicator has been the number of large services with branch museums that applied for later Marketing Consultancies and the good runout for the earlier workshops. The professional feedback from museums has been most encouraging. Curators have frequently told YHMC staff how useful and popular the booklet has been. The President of the Yorkshire & Humberside Federation wrote to express their appreciation of the project.

Perhaps the biggest and most quantifiable indicator to increased activity in this area has been seen through the production of a second Museums Alive! booklet in 1989 for distribution in 1990. Entries in the first booklet were free. To enable a second to be produced more income had to be generated. A obvious way was to charge a flat rate of £20.00 per entry per museum. Branch museums of larger services also paid £20.00. Members of the YHMC were informed of this in August 1989. *All* of the member museums agreed to pay this fee, from the smallest independent to the largest local authority. This is seen as positive proof that all museums in the region were affected by the campaign and have increased their marketing activity. For some it may be a modest step from a baseline of zero, for others it may be the germination of a larger long term marketing plan. Nevertheless, the result is that museums are now realising that marketing is something they can use, provided that it works with the aims and objectives of each individual institution. Museums Alive! has been seen by the membership as being of real benefit to them as a result they have been prepared, second time around, to pay for it. The broad coverage offered by such a joint initiative has been seen to be excellent value for money.

Museums Alive! into the 90's

Due to prudent financial management of the project it was realised that there would be enough money within the budget to produce a second booklet. This would be ready for the World Travel Market and distributed in a similar way to the first. It was agreed to double the print from 50,000 to 100,000. The estimated production cost was around £14,000 including distribution. YHMC Board of Management agreed to underwrite the project by £5,000.00. In addition to a grant of £530.00 from North Yorkshire County Council the actual production of £13,966.73 was able to be met.

The experience of producing the first booklet was of great benefit for the second edition. It appeared in time for the World Travel Market in December 1989 and the 100,000 were distributed to museums, TIC's etc. using the same channels as before.

The Museums Alive! project has enabled itself to project beyond 1989, Museums Year, with another high quality regional guide. This has been an unexpected addition to the project and can only help boost public awareness of museums and galleries within the region.

Conclusion

1. Marketing is something that museums have always done, even if they did not know it as such. Encouraging visitors, making them feel welcome, publicising the museum and its events, giving talks to groups are activities which museums are very familiar with. Even so, the times and circumstances continue to change and museums need to adapt to them and learn new skills when necessary.

2. The success of the project lay in a number of key areas. Firstly, in demystifying the concept of marketing and making it relevant to museum needs. The success of the booklets and the training through the Workshops and the 6 day course, illustrated that museum workers could see marketing as a useful tool for them. It was more than just publicity and it was a tool that they could control. It is our hope that marketing was something that could help their museum achieve its aims and that it was not something imposed on them by a hostile management and a consultant in a flash suit wielding a car-phone!

4. Secondly, it encouraged museums to consider how they should spend their publicity budgets, or if they should risk spending money on it at all! The six museums eligible for case studies will be able to work towards long term marketing plans. Those museums whose staff attended the 6 day course will have new skills to pass onto colleagues with regard to planning, targeting and monitoring marketing strategies. All will have seen the benefits of the booklet and leaflets.

Museums in Yorkshire and Humberside are moving towards the next century with increased confidence in their cultural and economic role in society. They are aware that the public increasingly demands quality. If it has done anything, Museums Alive! has shown that marketing is part of the drive for total quality in all areas of museum activity.

A VISITOR ATTENDANCE CONSULTANCY:

Ruddington Village Museum

Under the MGC one day marketing consultancy scheme, the Ruddington Village Museum called in Kathy Gee, then acting as an independent consultant, now Director of the West Midlands Area Museum Service. The museum's attendance figures doubled in 1990, sank a little in 1991, and are now climbing again. The curator welcomed the report, which she found full of useful suggestions.

The museum was founded in the Hermitage, the oldest building in the village situated behind the parish church. Part of the collections are still housed here. The remainder occupies space in St Peter's Rooms, a centrally sited public building.

The split site causes problems of staffing and due to its site, the Hermitage is sometimes missed. Both sites are leased, and both are insecure tenancies. Neither is large enough, nor could be extended to take the whole collection in one place. In addition, the Hermitage is environmentally unsuitable.

The immediate problem is the low visitor numbers achieved (1,357 at both sites in 1989). This is seen as a low return for the amount of volunteer effort expended.

Contributory factors

Any museum is not only influenced by its history. Other factors have shaped it too.

Geography:

Ruddington is a large village south of Nottingham. It is within easy reach of Derby and Leicester, but is not a tourist area. The village is a shopping centre for the surrounding area.

The village is also home to the Ruddington Framework Knitters Museum which has achieved some national acclaim. The existence of these two separate museums within the same small community is a mixed blessing.

Committee and management structure:

The Society is run by an executive committee. Interest in the museum is not universal and expenditure on the museum is cause for comment in some circles.

The museum has reached a crucial stage in its development. If it wishes to grow and give better service to a wider public, it can no longer be viewed as a subsidiary hobby of a faction within the society. The society should recognise the importance of what has been achieved and support its development wholeheartedly.

Staff and supporters:

The museum volunteers seem to have divided loyalties too! Strong emotional ties seem to exist to each building with the result that it is difficult to guide the museum in a particular direction. In the past, these 'political' problems have dictated museum policy, rather than an examination of the needs of the museum's visitors.

Advice and guidance:

The museum has had support from the East Midlands Museums Service and now has a Curatorial Adviser through Registration. As a result, they are aware of their curatorial problems even if they cannot solve them immediately.

Description of the museum

Museum buildings

The Hermitage:

The museum occupies a small part of this building. It is approached from the rear of the building, the entrance is not inviting or obvious. It is not clear whether the museum is open or closed. Access is difficult with a flight of steps hampering access by the disabled or elderly. The building is showing its age, dampness is a problem.

St Peter's Rooms:

Access to the whole building is at the back, through a passageway. To get to the museum, people have to go through other public institutions. Again, the entrance is not obvious or inviting. Access is good except for the temporary exhibitions room on the first floor. The building is suitable for museum use but is not large enough.

Internal arrangements

Neither building has room for a formal 'reception' desk or a sales point.

Both museums tell their stories within defined compartments. Thus the trade exhibits at St Peter's Rooms are in workshop settings, as is the Parlour at the Hermitage. This works quite well but there is no space for interpretation linking the different scenes. It would also be difficult to gather a history of the village from the displays as they are at present.

This technique is inevitable at the Hermitage due to the room layout, but St Peter's Rooms do offer scope for variation if desired.

Collections

The general public see the museum as a place, a building. But we know that collections are what make a museum. In terms of marketing, Ruddington's collection – the product – is good quality and has popular appeal.

Conservation standards are good.

Storage: there is almost adequate storage for the collection as it stands, but problems would arise with an expanding collection.

Display and interpretation

The display technique adopted is that of open display with room settings. It is attractive and effective.

Interpretation is almost entirely provided by the volunteers who act as guides. This produces good interaction with the public but does have some disadvantages. Training of the volunteers varies in quality. Visitors will inevitably be directed to the particular interests of the guide. The personal approach affects staffing levels as the guide cannot talk and act as a security system at the same time. If more casual visitors were to come, this system could cause problems, although it will probably always be the most effective for group visits.

The visitors

Your knowledge of who your visitors are, what they like, and what they want is based on observation and gut reaction. These are valid ways of assessing your visitors, but you would be well advised to glean more detailed information in the future.

At present, your visitors are almost entirely brought on organised group visits (31 groups, total 787 visitors in 1989). They have come because one of their number thought it was a good idea. The groups fall into two categories – child and adult with a majority of adults. Only 5 groups came from outside Nottinghamshire.

On the other hand, your casual visitor numbers are pitifully low. This is an indication of local use of the museum by individuals, as there are very few tourists to the village.

You tell me that the visitors thoroughly enjoy their visit – which I can well imagine. However, it would be interesting to find out what they liked best, and least, and what else they would like you to offer. Would they, for example, like toilets, catering, gift shop, gallery seating, information points, more labels? Do they find the sequence easy? Do they know where to go next? How long will it take? Are your staff thought welcoming, helpful and appropriate?

Community involvement

I have already highlighted the low number of casual visitors, which I interpret as a lack of local visitors. It is impossible to run a community museum without the support of the local community.

The Village Museum sets out to preserve and interpret everyday life within the community. As such, it differs from the Framework Knitter's museum in that it is not illustrating a specific technological process and the society which supported it. The Village Museum should, therefore have the support of the local community and it is strange that it appears to have a low profile. My guess is that it results from a) inconvenient opening hours and b) a perception that the museum is a private club for the History Society.

The public may see the Society as elitist (you have to be a member) and this rubs off onto the museum. I suggest that in future, you concentrate on getting the Museum's name into the press and so on, rather than the Society's. At the same time, you must put time and effort into cultivating contacts with other local societies, local authorities and special interest groups. Remember that personnel change, so do not rest on your laurels.

Finally, the Village Museum, as many others, was set up on a wave of enthusiasm. Maintaining that enthusiasm from a new generation of voluntary or paid staff is essential. Have you been successful?

Is there anyone out there who wants you?

This section is all about potential. To produce a realistic plan for the future you need to know what is going on in the outside world. We did not discuss this on the day, but you will find it a useful exercise to stop and look carefully at the 'market' in which you find yourselves.

In theory anyone who is not a current user of the museum is a potential future visitor. In practice people tend to fall into definable groups according to their needs.

Museums almost always find that they fall into at least four different 'market segments', so lets look at them separately.

Museums and special interests

This includes people who have a commitment to the arts, who are interested in heritage or the natural environment.

Look around you, can you identify groups in this category which might enjoy what you have to offer? How would you best contact them?

Museums and the community

Think about your 'community'. Is it increasing or shrinking? How could that affect you? Look at demographics – is yours a typical population or is there, say, a high proportion of children or pensioners?

Look at planning – are there plans for huge new housing or industrial estates? Will this produce more potential visitors?

Museums and education

Your museum has already got good contacts with educational groups, but could they be improved? Do your local schools visit regularly to do a variety of different topics or do they think you are only good for one subject? Exam courses are changing – how could your museum complement the new curricula? In which subjects? Think beyond history!

Museums and tourism

Tourists are just people who do not live in your area.
How many of them are there? Why are they in your area? Might they appreciate what you have to offer? How do you know?

Spend some time on desk research, your County and District Councils will have statistics of this sort. Talk to the Tourist Board.
Look at:

- Numbers, is this sector increasing or shrinking?

- People, do the surveys tell you anything about the types of people who visit your area and why? Are they the same sort of people who tend to like museums?

The Borough Council are keen to develop Ruddington as a tourist centre, see comments on the Country Park below. This is an opportunity which should be grasped actively.

Signposting and advertising

You already recognise that you have a problem with signs, both directional and on the building.

The brown signs cease at the car park where the Frameshop ones take over.

This gives them a head start.

Both Village Museum sites are unsignposted. The Hermitage has no permanent sign on the building or at the entrance to the car park. St Peter's Rooms does have a sign but it is so discrete as to be unnoticed.

Permanent signs within the village are important in raising awareness within the community.

Temporary signs, for use when the museum is open, should be eyecatching and professionally produced. they should reflect the quality of what is to be seen within.

Advertising is limited by your budget but you have been successful in getting free publicity. However, guide books have limited success.

A fee leaflet is certainly the most important piece of print you can buy. The existing leaflet is elegant but short on information and rather wasteful of space. To economise, leave the Frameshops out, reduce the leaflet to $\frac{1}{3}$rd A4 in size and print in larger quantities.

When considering distribution try to target to a particular geographical region, social group, age group, or interest group. Do not just issue leaflets and hope that the right people find them.

Competition

Your major 'problem' is the Framework Knitter's Museum. It has a national name and has a good profile locally. Ironically, the two organisations should not really be seen as in conflict – they merely reflect two different aspects of local history. However, in a village of 7,000 inhabitants, serving say another 7,000 in the area, any attraction which gets 6,000 visitors a year must represent competition.

They have a head start – they show people at work, their opening hours are convenient and they have a more than local story to tell.

One should also note the development of the Country Park within one mile of the village. this will also provide a terminus for a steam railway. The distance is such that the village may not benefit directly from the changes, indeed it may suffer.

Making the future happen

It is at this point that we begin to think laterally/ Look at the markets you have identified, how can you change and develop your museum so that it satisfies the needs of both present *and* potential users?

Development potential

Before we go any further we must be realistic. Does the museum have real potential to develop its service? The answer is definitely yes.

The collections and displays deserve wider recognition and can certainly be used to greater effect. Those groups which use the museum already represent only a fraction of your potential.

There appear to be two avenues to explore:

a. Increase group visits.

b. Develop the casual visitor trade.

It would be possible to limit the museum's activities to pre-booked group visits only. This would be labour-effective as volunteers would be guaranteed work to do. On the other hand it would restrict local access.

I believe that your greatest field for expansion is in casual visitors. These will be locals, their families and friends.

However, the Society would recognise that 'more people means more work' – an increase in visitor numbers will mean a radical rethink of a) sites, b) staffing, c) display technique.

Displays

It should be a priority to get all the displays together under one roof. There are three options at present a) St Peter's Rooms, b) the Hermitage and c) the Country Park. It is too early to make a choice and there are already factions appearing. In order to avoid this, and to ensure the best result FOR THE VISITOR, a group should agree on a list of minimum criteria which the new museum should fulfil. This list will then act as a check for each site in turn.

As already suggested, a visitor survey should be undertaken and then the information you have gathered from your visitors about their likes and dislikes should be used when you come to review your displays.

In the immediate future, consideration should be given to methods of interpreting the exhibits which do not rely on guide volunteers. Similarly, if less volunteers are to be on duty due to longer opening hours, the security of the exhibits needs to be reviewed.

Marketing the result

So far I have suggested changes in the museum based on your knowledge of the market – what the marketing men would call 'improving the product'. But those changes will not affect anything if the public do not know about them.

It is probably impossible to communicate effectively with all consumer groups. So target. Do it before you decide which type of communication to use.

Identify markets to be targeted

a. Local community

b. Educational groups

c. Adult groups

Set visitor targets annually

Do take account of special exhibitions and other events. Note special new initiatives each year.
Check regularly to see if your changes are having an effect.

Agree pricing policies annually

Your major decision is related to the museum's standing within the society. To what extent is it necessary for the museum to pay its way? Or will the society underwrite its losses as part of its role in 'researching and disseminating' information about Ruddington's history?
It has been argued that the main priority is to ensure that more people benefit from the museum. Pricing is a crucial factor here. You should consider special concessions for groups which you wish to encourage.
Options include:

Price reductions for school groups.

Charging for pre-booked groups but combining it with other reduced options.

Free admission to locals on production of proof.

Special family tickets.

Review your opening hours annually

In view of your somewhat unusual opening hours, one wonders whether they are designed to be convenient to YOU or the public?
Following discussions the following suggestion was made by the group present on the one day consultancy:
Pre-booked groups – open by appointment.
Tues – Sat, 10–12.

We were anxious to give access to people who are at work during the week, school children doing individual research and the unwaged.

Undertake visitor surveys annually

Without a survey you will never really know what your visitors think, want or appreciate. this need not be a very complicated affair – EMMS can probably advise you.

Renew relationships with local interest groups annually

Identify local and community groups which could be expected to support the museum and to become involved in it. Think about: Rotary et al, Women's Institutes, evening classes, groups with special physical needs and other local societies. Specify the ways in which you intend to contact them, enlist and maintain their interest, and exploit the opportunities which they offer.

The types of things that work are: offering lectures, special openings, seeking their specialist knowledge, joint activities.

Education

You already have fairly good relationships with schools. But you could still attract others – the local Education Advisers are usually very keen to help. Do use the County's internal mailing system to deliver leaflets – but they will be most effective if they are advertising specific events or services rather than general information.

Tourism

It would be unrealistic to expect the Village Museum to make significant inroads into the tourist market when working alone. The village is not, yet, a recognised stopping point. This must be the first move and can only be achieved by County or District Authorities – make sure that they know they have your support.

If the District does go ahead with its plans, you should really join in wholeheartedly, money 'risked' in this area will almost certainly reap dividends if it is part of a major scheme.

Joint action is the key here.

A media campaign

Every change at the museum is worth a story. If a development plan is adopted then there are innumerable opportunities for media interest. Do not slow down once the schemes are underway or flag towards the end! Work out the new contacts you intend to make.

Remember to make sure that these changes are under the banner of the Museum (not the Society). It is the Museum's profile which needs to rise and the public can be confused if it is linked to the governing body which has a different name.

Services

Sales:

Your sales range reflects the interests of the Society rather than the needs of your visitors. I know that you have limited space but a small range of quality 'souvenir items, or books (try the Shire Albums range), adds to visitor enjoyment. The stock control and finances are seen to be a problem I know, but they really need not be. Make sure that one person is responsible, and give them due credit for the results of their labours.

You could expect to sell 30p per head. As the normal mark up on books is 33% the sums would work out at something like:

1000 visitors x 30p = £300

Investment   = £200

Profit   = £100

Publications:

This is also part of marketing – providing extra information to those that want it. The society's publications programme is adventurous, but I was not clear whether it was planned in response to public demand or was just what happened to interest you. Try to identify subjects for which you know there is a demand – sales will be higher.

Customer comfort:

You are in rather poor supply here! The absence of toilets is a genuine problem, particularly for school groups, but I can see no solution. However, when considering any future move, add toilets and seating areas, to your list of requirements.

The staff

I visited under unusual circumstances and so cannot tell from first had experience whether your staff are welcoming, helpful and friendly, but I suspect that they are! The main thing to watch here is their training. This especially applies to guides who can give wrong information in a misguided effort to please just by saying something.

There is a clear need to build up a team spirit in volunteers at the Village Museum. You could do this by having special events for them alone – probably including an element of training. An induction session twice a year would help, combined perhaps with the occasional meeting where a curator from another museum is asked to speak.

If you extend the opening hours as suggested you will have to either a) find more Stewards or b) rationalise the use of existing volunteers. A third option could be the offer of an honorarium to the volunteer's efforts to dealing directly with the public in guiding.

The museum is, however, holding significant collections and you should give long term thought to its care. There could be a case for employing a part time, professionally qualified curator to assist in the running and marketing of the museum. This professionalism could be purchased on an hourly basis from a self employed curator, or could be provided on a District basis by a peripatetic curator employed by the Borough to support museums within its area.

Exhibitions

This is a prime area for involving the local community. In addition to your own internally generated exhibitions, get other groups to participate. Offer them space -their families and friends will want to come and will have to see the museum en route.

When thinking about subject areas – again, think of the visitor first. Are there subjects which you know link in with schools' TV series for example. Identify popular subjects for future exhibitions which are within your capabilities to resource. Describe the target audience for each subject.

Advertising

Paid advertising in guide books and newspapers is probably beyond your budget and is, in any case, of limited effect in small quantities. Concentrate your resources into bright, well designed attractive leaflets and their effective distribution.

Plan to change your leaflet every season – even if only by changing the colour ink in which it is printed. When choosing a design, remember who you are targeting a) your existing public and b) your potential public.

Signposting and signage

As referred to earlier in this report – this is an area for improvement .

Entrance features

Your entrances are easy to miss – but in the present premises this is difficult to improve. This is a crucial area for improvement – you will not get casual trade if people find it difficult to get in. Either negotiate with the landlords for better access, or recognise the problems and continue to search for other premises.

A LARGE MUSEUM MARKETING PLAN

MANCHESTER MUSEUM OF SCIENCE AND INDUSTRY

MARKETING PLAN

This museum is one of the fastest growing museums in the country. It has an unusual mixture of funding, part coming from central government, and from other sources – largely self-generated. The museum has a regularly revised corporate plan in which marketing plans play an important part. Targets are set each year, as part of a three year planning cycle. Regular market research is a key element in every aspect of planning, and the customer care policy is related to this. The marketing plan is followed by a report on customer care development within the museum.

INTRODUCTION

1. This report presents details of the new Marketing Plan for the Museum of Science and Industry for the next two years (1991–1993). As the role of marketing within the Museum continues to develop, a strategic marketing planning process has been adopted. This ensures that all marketing activities are directed at realising the objectives in the Museum's Corporate Plan, and reflect its role in the marketplace

2. Previous Marketing Plans have tended to concentrate on broad based task-centred activities on a year by year basis in line with an increased investment in the Department. The new Marketing Plan takes a longer term view of Marketing and Development issues which is more in keeping with the Museum's philosophy of long-term strategic corporate planning. The increased investment in resources, in staffing levels and the marketing budget, will facilitate a more pro-active approach which will meet the needs of the Museum in the 1990s. The proposed budget allocation for the financial year 1991/1992 is £120,000, which will be invested in a programme of activities outlined in section E of this report.

BACKGROUND

3. In developing the Marketing Plan, as well as the individual strategies which will be included in it, it is essential to incorporate information relating to the Museum's Corporate Objectives (as outlined in the new Corporate Plan). The findings of the recent Market Research Survey also provide essential information regarding existing visitor profiles as well as presenting a clear picture of awareness levels and perception in the Greater Manchester region. This data together with other external factors influencing the Museum's development will be used to inform decisions on marketing strategies for the future.

EXTERNAL FACTORS

4. The strategic marketing planing process requires an approach which takes into account the external environment as well as internal product-centred developments. It is essential that visitor levels are increased if the Museum is to attain the targets set out in the new Corporate Plan. It must be recognised, however, that the Museum is operating in an increasingly competitive marketplace where the resources available in terms of government funding, admissions income and visitor spending are now being distributed across an even broader base than in previous years.

5. This report cannot provide a comprehensive study of the current economic situation, however a number of issues must be considered in assessing the potential for increasing (and maintaining) visitor numbers and visitor spending at the Museum. These issues include the current economic situation as well as the changing demographic profile of the UK population. (See report from Henley Centre for Forecasting at Appendix 1).

6. Victor Middleton in his recent study (New Visions for Independent Museums) has analysed the socio-economic trends which will influence Museum visiting in the next decade. He points out that leisure spending is discretionary and Museums in general are competing not just with other Museums but also visitor attractions, theme parks, retail and cinema entertainment such as computer games and video stores.

7. This increasing competition, as well as the changes in the demographic profile of the population will influence activities across a range of areas, including the development of new galleries which continue to meet the needs of visitors.

15. Royal Museum of Scotland Restaurant, Edinburgh.

8. The changes in the profile of the UK population will mean that between 1990 and 1995 the 15–24 year age group will *decrease* by 25% whilst the 45–54 year age group will *increase* by the same percentage. This means that the 90s will see a trend of marketing to more mature age groups (away from the youth-orientated marketing of the 1980s). There will also be an increase in the number of young families as the 'baby boomers' of the 1960s have children of their own.

9. The implications of these trends for the Museum of Science and Industry is that in the short term, the main category of visitors (family groups, parents aged 25–45) will not be significantly affected. However long term marketing plans must address the issue of the changing population. It is essential that resources are used to the best advantage and that existing campaigns aim to 'fill the gaps' in the Museum's visitor profile, particularly amongst more mature visitors and the 15–24 age group.

10. Future marketing activities will continue to monitor the noted above so that the Marketing Department is able to respond to changes quickly and efficiently. A flexible response to demographic changes and an awareness of visitor needs will be a central theme in strategic planning throughout the Museum.

MARKET RESEARCH RESULTS

11. The 1988 Market Research indicated that 78% of visitors were derived from the Greater Manchester, Lancashire and Cheshire regions. In 1990 the proportion of visitors from this geographical area is similar (80%), however there has been a marked increase in the proportion of visitors from Cheshire. This fact, coupled with the relatively high awareness levels in South Manchester seems to indicate high levels of success in previous marketing and public relations activity in this area. Future marketing activity must build on this strength and at the same time address those areas which have lower levels of awareness and provide fewer visitors to the Museum.

12. The socio-economic grouping of visitors is also highlighted within the summary document. The Museum is very successful in attracting a broad audience (particularly in comparison to the national profile of Museum visitors).

13. The proportion of visitors in the 'AB' category has seen a marked increase in the last two years, from 25% of visitors in 1988 to 43% in 1990. This increase must be contributing factor to the overall increase in visitor numbers during this period, particularly since the proportion of visitors in other categories has slightly declined.

14. The proportion of 'C2DE' visitors has changed from 39% of total visitors in 1988 to 27% of total visitors in 1990. Since the overall number of visitors to the Museum has increased by 37.8% in this period, the slight decrease in percentage terms in the C2DE group does not in fact appeal to all audiences and it is essential that the visitor profile of the Museum reflects the profile of the general population as far as possible. Future marketing activities will address the issue of socio-economic grouping so that targeted events and specific media are used to best effect in addressing particular audiences.

15. The recent survey also highlights a significant increase in one category of visitors to the museum. There has been a marked increase in the 33–44 year age group (from 29% in 1988 to 41% in 1990). This factor, coupled with the very high proportion of visitors with children (61%) reflects the Museum's strength in

providing a popular family-based day out. The strength of this appeal provides a basis for future media campaigns.

16. The proportion of visitors in the 55 plus age group is still very low (11% of Museum visitors) compared to the profile of the North West population (33% of the total North West population). This fact, coupled with the change in the population over the next ten years (see section B of this report) presents an opportunity for future targeted campaigns, particularly for groups in the older age range.

17. The Museum is now drawing from a much broader catchment area than in previous years. In 1988, 18% of visitors had travelled more than thirty miles whereas in 1990 this figure had increased to 24% of total visitors. Increased media presence and more effective distribution of Museum literature, as well as personal recommendation to visit, are all significant factors in developing the reputation of the Museum throughout the North West and beyond.

MARKETING OBJECTIVES

18. Specific, quantified objectives for the Marketing Department for the period 1991–1993 consistent with the Corporate Plan are as follows:-

1991–1992
To consolidate the 40% growth seen in 1990 and aim for an increase in visitor levels by 6% to 350,000.
To maintain existing levels of business in the conference centre and to generate an income of £28,000 (facility hire).

1992–1993
To increase visitor levels by 5.7% to 370,000.
To increase conference income to £29,400 (Room hire only).

19. Other basic objectives which are fundamental to the development of the Museum's marketing activities are as follows:-

To continue to raise awareness of the Museum among its various publics, particularly in target groups identified in the communications plan.
To maximise revenues through admission charges and visitor spend.
To create and convert opportunities for sponsorship.
To monitor and evaluate all marketing activities and ensure maximum return on investment in all areas.
To develop efficient methods of evaluating visitor perceptions so that new developments can take into account visitor needs and expectations.

20. **Advertising agency**
A number of options have been considered including the use of a full service Advertising Agency and/or Media Buying Specialists and individual Design companies. It is recommended that, as in recent months, any future arrangement with outside agencies is approached on a project-by-project basis so that a flexible approach can be adopted.

21. **Media schedule**
Advertising activity in 1990 has centred on highlighting individual events such as 'Out of this World' and 'Everyone's A Winner'. The majority of the media coverage

has been generated by extensive PR activities. In order to build on the success of last year's PR campaign, an even higher profile media campaign will be developed over the next two years.

22. This will include advertising in key publications in the fields of tourism, education and conferences. In 1991/2 the majority of investment will focus on a well-planned local and regional media campaign, particularly concentrating on areas around Greater Manchester which are shown to have lower awareness i.e. to the North and East of the city. In 1992/3 subject to the results of further market research, advertising activity will focus on a broader geographical area, across the whole of the North West. The media schedule will also take into account the issue of targeting particular groups of visitors e.g. family groups, the 15–24 year age group and more mature sections of the population.

23. The 'motivation to visit' factor is obviously a central issue in the development of this year's Media Schedule. The majority of visitors (67%) to the Museum make their decisions to visit on the day or the day before their actual visit. Tactical advertising will be closely assessed to obtain the most cost effective means of reaching potential and existing customers. It is also proposed that an outdoor poster campaign be included in the new schedule, particularly in terms of raising the Museum of Science and Industry profile in the city centre.

24. **Public relations programme**
The increased awareness levels highlighted in the recent survey as well as the increasing number of visitors to the Museum indicate that recent PR activities have been very successful in raising awareness. The amount of media coverage in local, regional and national press and TV has increased dramatically over the last two years.

25. A planned PR Programme will maximise opportunities provided by major events at the Museum, including:-

Energy for Future Exhibition;
The Planet Project;
The Opening of the Gas Gallery.

The Museum is working closely with British Gas North West in implementing a PR campaign of a year's duration. Already this is producing dividends in the form of press, radio and television coverage.

26. The Museum's well-established links with local and regional media will be developed further, ensuring coverage wherever possible of events and news items throughout the year. The PR programme will also aim to take advantage of all opportunities to target specific groups of visitors in specialist and trade publications.

27. The Daily Telegraph 'Out of this World' competition and the 'Everyone's a Winner' competition have proved very successful in generating coverage, by press and TV, across a national and a regional base. Plans are now under way to develop a third Daily Telegraph national competition, in partnership with British Gas, which will serve as an excellent means pre-publicity for the Gas Gallery.

28. **Printwork and distribution**
The recent survey highlights of success of the extended distribution of leaflets in the last twelve months (45% of those recalling publicity for Museum of Science and

Industry). The extended services, as well as the increased number of visitors for the Museum has resulted in an even greater demand for the quantity and range of printwork required. The existing leaflet serves as a guide to the site as well as a promotional tool.

29. In 1991 a new style of promotional leaflet will be produced incorporating a special events calender. As in recent years individual flyers and programmes will be designed to highlight specific events. The special events calender will provide an opportunity for direct mailing to target groups and also serve as a forward planner for group organisers.

30. The needs of visitors on site will be accommodated by a comprehensive plan of the site including all details on visitor services etc. This will be supplemented by additional information points throughout the site in the form of videos, graphic panels and information boards.

31. The range of foreign language leaflets, currently available French, Italian, German, and Spanish will be extended to cover other languages. The emphasis on the availability of literature in other languages is in keeping with the Museum's intention to offer a service to an international as well local visitors.

32. ***Special events and temporary exhibitions***

As in recent years, the programme of special events at the Museum will be developed in order to present new and changing perspectives to visitors. The Special Events Programme not only provides specific activities for specialist interest groups, but it also offers repeat visitors to the Museum the chance to be involved in new activities. The recent survey showed that 44% of those questioned were either visiting the Museum for a second time or were in fact regular visitors each year. It is essential that the existing customer base is retained and that repeat visiting is actively encouraged.

33. The range of galleries and themes available in the site is extensive. In the next years, in conjunction with other departments, it is intended to develop a new programme of events and exhibitions which build on the more innovative and interactive themes within the Museum. A programme of science shows, children's workshops and open evenings is planned as a pilot scheme for 1991. The success of these new ideas and the feedback from visitors will be reviewed at the end of the year so that in 1992 the programme can be developed.

34. Special events and temporary exhibitions also offer the opportunity to target specific groups of the community, particularly the locally based groups and groups of different cultural origins which make up such a high proportion of the population of the area around the Museum.

35. ***Market research***

It is essential to continue to develop a clear picture of the Museum from the perspective of existing and potential visitors. This will assist in the preparation of future marketing plans as well as the development of the corporate planning process, and has implications for all Museum developments. The setting of realistic and achievable targets and objectives is fundamental to the success of this approach.

In the short term it is essential that the needs and expectations of existing and potential visitors are analysed.

36. The recent survey highlighted a number of areas where development is required, however it is necessary to introduce a second stage of research which will probe further into the main points highlighted. This qualitative research will provide information on a range of issues including the perceptions of the Museum amongst existing visitors and also amongst those who would not consider visiting museums at all.

37. Attitudes of existing printwork, advertisements and the collections themselves will be examined so that future activity can take into account central themes which could affect the development of visitor levels and visiting patterns. Repeat visiting is a key factor in the recent increase in visitor numbers. It is important that the Museum does not lose sight of the visitor as a 'consumer' – more sophisticated, well educated and with high expectations of customer care and service. The Museum has a strong commitment to customer care; a high quality product and the maintenance of standards are of paramount importance if repeat visiting and recommendation are to continue to develop.

38. In addition to the qualitative research mentioned above, which will be provided by an external agency, it is intended to introduce a series of in-house visitor surveys during the next two years which will supplement the information already available.

39. In terms of assessing public awareness, a survey will be commissioned in 1992 which will re-examine levels of awareness in the areas throughout Greater Manchester. An additional survey will assess awareness levels at satellite points throughout the North West in order to assess and evaluate marketing and PR initiatives with a view to extending the range of campaigns in future years. Monitoring and evaluation of all activities will continue to play a central role in the development of future strategies.

40. *Exhibitions*

The Museum will continue to take advantage of opportunities provided by local and national exhibitions which are aimed at the general public, trade and conference buyers.

A number of portable exhibits are being built by the Xperiment! team which will present an unusual attraction for the Museum's stand at future exhibitions. This year the Museum will be represented at the following exhibitions:-

February	Confex	An international exhibition for the conference market
February	NWTB	Heritage Workshop – aimed at group organisers
April	MOOT	The National exhibition for coach and tour operators
April	Tameside Education Resource Centre	Exhibition for school groups
June	The Cheshire Show	
June	G Mex	Northern Conference and Hospitality Show
August	The National Eisteddfod of Wales	

41. **Joint promotional activities** The Museum will play an active role in the development of initiatives by the following organisations:-
    Greater Manchester Visitor and Convention Bureau
    The North West Tourist Board
    Arts About Manchester
    The English Tourist Board
    The British Tourist Authority

42. **Metrolink** The opening of the Metrolink light rapid transport system will considerably improve public transport access to Castlefield. There is potential for Metrolink to be marketed as an easy way of getting to the Museum.

43. **Conferences** The development of the Museum's Conference Centre and the promotion and co-ordination of conferences and events will remain an essential role for the Marketing Department in the next two years. The Museum now has a well established base of conference customers with a high level of satisfaction for the services offered.

    Attendance at exhibitions, advertisements in key publications and direct mail will continue to develop awareness of the Museum's facilities. Levels of service will be monitored to ensure that the well-established reputation of the Conference Centre is maintained in the future.

CONCLUSION

44. Since the establishment of a Marketing Department within the Museum in 1987, the increased investment in both staff and resources has continued to pay dividends in the form of a higher public profile, increased media coverage, a growth in awareness levels and increased visitor numbers. The new Marketing Plan reflects the continued commitment to a range of marketing and PR activities which play a crucial role in the development of the Museum as defined in the Corporate Plan.

    The development of new exhibitions, special events and temporary exhibitions provides a framework for a planned, pro-active campaign. This will build on existing awareness levels, encourage repeat visits and address those target groups of the population which are not represented within the current profile of visitors to the Museum.

    Attendance at exhibitions aimed at the conference and travel trade, group organisers and the general public will provide promotional opportunities across a range of target groups, both regionally and in some cases on a national scale.

    Monitoring and evaluation of current activities as well as regular reviews of individual campaigns will ensure the most effective investment of resources in terms of staff time, media spending and PR activities. The Marketing Plan itself will be reviewed on an annual basis to ensure the realisation of the Museum's corporate aims and objectives.

A SMALL MUSEUM MARKETING PLAN

REGIMENTS OF GLOUCESTER MUSEUM 1993–1994

WHY?

To attract 16,000 visitors in FY 1993–1994

WHAT?

The Product:

An enjoyable, entertaining and educational visit to the Regiments of Gloucestershire Museum

FOR WHOM?

Target Markets:

Local population
Day trippers and tourists to Gloucester City and Docks

HOW?

Pricing
Advertising
Mailshots
Publicity
Trade exhibitions
Trading
Special services: for schools, lectures, evening visits
Special events and exhibitions
Signposting
Market Research
Image

Market Segments

Men, women and children of all ages
    Serving soldiers and families
    Old Comrades and families
    Gloucester residents
    Gloucestershire residents
    Bristol and Avon residents
    Schools and colleges in Gloucestershire and Avon
    Clubs and societies (local and regional)
    Day trippers to the Docks
    Day trippers to Gloucester
    Tourists to the Cotswolds
    Tourists to the Forest of Dean
    Military enthusiasts
    Coach parties

Resources
Financial: Budget 100%

An award-winning museum
Human: Staff
               Friends
               Volunteers
               Battalion/Regiment
Time (not enough)
Goodwill
Marketing partnerships
Sponsorship

THE PLAN

1. PRICING

Competitive in relation to other museums in the Docks
Adult: 2.50   OAP: 1.50   Child 1.25   Family: 6.25

*   cheaper than the National Waterways Museum (a shorter visit). Admission
    charges for 1993 (TBC) :
Adult: 3.75   OAP/Child: 2.75   Family: 9.50

*   more expensive than the Opie Collection (more varied displays). Admission
    charges for 1991:
Adult: 1.95   OAP: 1.50   Child: 75p   Family: 4.95

2. ADVERTISING

Drip feed
Bursts?

Drip feed:	*How*	*Where?*	*When?*	*How much?*
	Leaflets	Gloucestershire and HETB area TICs Museums Hotels Guest houses	Continuous	42% (printing)
	Listings Museum guides Conference guides Coach operators School guides Specialist guides	Tourist guide	Continuous	29%

Drip feed:	*How?*	*Where?*	*When?*	*How much?*
	Photo displays	Museum shop ACO, AYT Trade Fairs	Continuous	5%

Bursts

	How?	*Where?*	*When?*	*How much?*
	Press releases Advertising	Local and regional press Radio	Half-terms Easter Hols Aug Bank Hol Events Major new acquisitions	6%

3. MAILSHOTS

Specially produced information sheets mailed to   5%
     schools (local and regional)
     specialist groups/societies (local and regional)
     coach operators (Midlands, Northwest, Northeast, Wales)

4. PUBLICITY

Press releases to
     local and regional press
     local radio and TV
     museums publications
     armed forces publications
     specialist topics publications eg.
     military models
     military history
     holiday
     leisure

Good public relations, especially with *Gloucester City Tourism Department* which is committed to promoting all attractions in the city. Funding partnerships and personal contributions to some projects for maximum impact.

Docks Trading Company which organises and funds events to attract visitors to the area. Funding partnerships.

The local media.

5. TRAVEL TRADE EXHIBITIONS AND PUBLIC SHOWS   6%

Selling the museum to the public on a personal basis.
     Cheltenham/Bristol Holiday Shows
     Swindon Travel Fair
     Heart of England Tourist Board Outings Fair

6. TRADING / MERCHANDISING

Offer the visitor a competitively-priced and interesting selection of well presented goods
linked to the museum's collections and displays
> books
> educational material
> gifts
> souvenirs
> specialist stock (regimental/military)

7. SPECIAL SERVICES

For schools
> Twilight and Inset training sessions for teachers
> teachers' pre-visit information packs
> teachers' resource packs
> activity and discovery sessions

Evening visits for groups by appointment
> lectures
> away from the museum
> in the museum

8. SPECIAL EVENTS

In the Docks with the support of the regiments:
> band concerts
> marching displays
> vehicle and weapon displays

In the museum
> eg children's weekend and holiday activities
> special exhibitions

NB. None planned at present due to lack of resources

9. SIGNAGE   2%

Ensure that effective directional and locational signs are properly maintained by City
Council and Docks Co.

Display effective signs at Custom House

Case Study

10. IMAGE

We must
    be aware of our visitors' expectations and needs
    be efficient
    be welcoming
    observe our in-house customer care code
    provide value for money

11. SUMMARY

Total Budget

Leaflet printing	42%
Listings	29%
Photography/printing	5%
Press/radio advertising	6%
Mailshots	5%
Travel shows	6%
Signage	2%
Spare/contingency	5%

CREATING A CLIMATE FOR CUSTOMER CARE

J PATRICK GREENE, Director, Museum of Science & Industry, Manchester

This describes a sequence of events that have contributed towards a climate for customer care within the Museum of Science and Industry in Manchester. It should be emphasised that our campaign is far from finished, and we have much still to achieve. Indeed, I would argue that a subject such as customer care is not one which is capable of being 'finished' – it is more analogous to a lubricant that helps the organisation run smoothly but which requires topping up on a continuing basis. The final point to make in introducing this paper is that although ours is a comparatively large museum with 107 staff, five buildings underlying our programme are applicable to an organisation of any size.

This case study covers the past two years. In the Autumn of 1989 the Museum held one of its annual Management Forum residential training courses – two days spent away from the museum in which all 13 managers participate in aspects of management training, and at the same time develop an area of policy. Our first step was to clarify what we meant by customer care. For us, a major step forward was the realisation that customer care extended far beyond the interaction between paying visitors with front-of-house staff, to cover all contacts between people working for the museum, and *everyone* with whom they came into contact in the course of their work. That introduced the concept of customer care as a shared responsibility of the entire museum staff, and was an essential pre-requisite for every subsequent action, including the development of a policy statement.

The other achievement of the two days was a rigorous exercise in self criticism, for which previous team-building programmes were important. Criticism can all too easily become divisive and wounding, so an atmosphere of trust in which colleagues address the weaknesses in the performance of the organisation as matters of *corporate* responsibility is essential. A consolidated list of twenty areas for improvement was produced, with an action list of individuals responsible for taking them forward. Managers proved themselves prepared to tackle topics outside their usual area of responsibility – for example, the knowledge that for many (especially older) visitors there were not enough places to sit down, revealed in visitor surveys, led to research by our archivist who scoured the museum site for possible locations for additional seating. A topic that I adopted was the need for pathways across the stone seats that cover most of our site for use by disabled visitors, the need for which had been demonstrated in visitor surveys and also by a wheelchair bound member of our friends' organisation. To cut a long story short, this scheme was completed a year ago thanks to an ADAPT grant, for which we are very grateful to the Carnegie U.K. Trust – a gratitude shared by all our visitors with walking difficulties, by parents pushing child carriers, and by staff moving trolleys loaded with equipment across the site. Those two items, seating and paths, are physical improvements to the museum. Other topics included language training, to be tackled through the training programme, to an awareness-raising experience in which every manager spent a day working on the main reception desk in the museum entrance.

Action plans are all very well, but without follow-up not enough will happen. We therefore monitored progress at subsequent meetings of our Management Forum, which meets on a monthly basis for half a day. Inclusion of a number of key initiatives within the Corporate Plan was also essential.

16. *Print Room of the Ashmolean Museum, Oxford.*

In December 1990 another follow-up activity took place – a one day course involving all managers and their deputies, a total of 21 people. Further work took place on developing the policy, and examining organisational performance. We found that of the 20 areas for action identified the previous year, 17 had been completed or had seen significant progress. Workshop groups during the day identified another 34 areas for improvement and again delegated topics to groups of 2 or 3 people in each case. These are some of the concerns:

- Condition and use of Baby Change and First Aid Rooms
- Need for a picnic area
- Car parking provision
- Condition of the streets surrounding the museum
- Name badges for staff and Friends, volunteers and trustees
- Evaluation and monitoring of visitors' experience and perceptions.

This last item is of particular significance, in moving away from a reactive approach to customer care (which is what I have described so far) to a much more anticipatory approach. This has now fed into the Marketing Plan, to be presented to our Trustees later this month, which addresses the issues through market research in two ways:

- Focus groups, looking at the Museum as a whole.
- Audience advocacy, concentrating on particular gallery developments and with target groups.

In March this year a review of progress with all the initiatives took place, and will be repeated again before the end of this year. By March it was possible to frame a draft Customer Care Policy for the museum, which will be taken for endorsement to a future meeting of the Board of Trustees.

So to summarise: over the first year and a half of the programme, action took place in two principal ways:

1. Ensuring that there was full managerial commitment to customer care by involving all managers initially, and then involving their deputies to gain their support; and

2. Taking action across a wide range of activities to make sure that results of the initiatives would have an immediate impact thereby emphasising that this was not a paper exercise.

During that period however, the most significant advance was made by integrating customer care into the Museum's training programme. As a result all staff have access to training that can improve their performance in their job – for example through public speaking workshops, foreign language courses, and seminars addressing the issues of communicating with visitors through exhibition techniques. Specific courses on customer care have been made available to, for example, attendant staff and demonstrators. Like the courses for managers, these include sessions of self criticism of the organisation. Earlier this year customer care tailored to the needs of the attendants resulted in a Customer Care Action Plan with 18 points identified. About half of the areas for improvement have been completed or have resulted in significant advances. The Action Plan has a completion date of 1 March 1992.

A valuable by-product of all this activity is the development of standards against which performance can be judged. In catering this included food handling, appearance, table-clearing etc. We have also introduced a customer complaints procedure relating to every person in the museum. This has formalised the reporting the reporting of complaints, thus enabling swifter action to be taken in addressing them. The mid-term training plan has customer care as one of its key development projects.

Performance is measured in a number of ways – the complaints procedure, market research, letters from visitors, press coverage and judges' remarks in competitions.

My final note is this – customer care has to be part of the culture of the organisation, in which it is an instinctive part of the behaviour of every member of staff, the volunteers, and the trustees. As I mentioned at the beginning, it is a challenge which never ceases. Even if you have addressed every conceivable need of visitors, and even if every person who comes into contact with them is fully trained and committed, the visitors themselves will change, their needs and interests will vary, their numbers will fluctuate, the museum will alter and so on. Changing the climate requires an irreversible change in the entire approach of the museum – a climatic change like a benign greenhouse effect, in which every person using the museum feels the warmth in the atmosphere.

DEVISING YOUR MARKETING PLAN

by Gerri Morris

With assistance from the Museums & Galleries Commission, the North West Museums Service produced a booklet called 'Marketing Planning for Museums and Galleries'. This extract is a synopsis of an effective approach to preparing a marketing plan, especially for that moment when you are first considering the structure and preparation of your plan – in fact, wondering how to do it.

WHO ARE WE, WHAT ARE WE HERE FOR?

The answers to these questions have to be the first step in devising your marketing plan. Reviewing the basis purpose of your organisation, its stated policy and what it is trying to achieve are inextricably linked to -

HOW WELL ARE WE DOING?

To review the performance of your museum or gallery requires a marketing audit. The first stage of this is known as a situational analysis, ie an analysis of your current situation. Done properly it takes time, but gives you invaluable information for the future management of your organisation.

The situational analysis requires a critical review of the following:

1. The Organisation

Statement of mission – or basis purpose of the organisation.
Aims – how the mission will be achieved.
Objectives – actual goals for achievement.

2. The Product

The subject matter; quality of displays and exhibits; the site and its buildings; quality of interpretative material; interpretive and interactive processes involved; quality of customer care; knowledge and manner of guides and attendants; atmosphere and ambience.
Facilities: shop and merchandise; publications; research and education facilities; toilet facilities; access and parking; cafe, restaurant, refreshments.

Activity programme; extra events; craft fairs; exhibitions etc.
     You are reviewing anything that can affect the experience of the attender.

3. Income

Income by attendances; grant-aid; sponsorship; education; cafe; merchandise; services; special events.

These figures need to cover at least the last three years, if not longer. You are looking for trends, are figures rising or falling, are they rising in places and falling in others? Can you explain the trends?

4. Attendances

You need to give annual figures for as many years as you can, by year and by month, even by weather conditions. Have figures gone up or down or stabilised? Which months are the busiest, which are the quietest? If you can, list attendances by days of the week and again watch the trends – are you actually closing on a day when you might attract good business? Is the day you thought was your quietest actually so?

5. The Market

Attenders: This requires audience surveys, but it is worth the effort. A survey can tell you who your attenders are; where they travel from; who they come with; what made them come; how long they stayed; what they liked best about their visit; how they found out about you.

This is all crucial information to your marketing plan: knowing who already comes can help you identify the markets you need to attract in the future; knowing what makes them come tells you which publicity method is most effective, and where you are wasting money. Knowing what they like best tells you whether you are promoting the features of your venue that mean the most to people.

Competition: Which organisations do you see yourself as being in competition with? How many similar organisations are competing for the public's leisure time? What are their resources like in relation to yours? How do their visitor numbers compare? There is more to be gained from collaboration with similar venues, but you nevertheless need to consider the effect of competition.

6. Potential Market

Having looked at who exactly is coming, now is your opportunity to look to see who you might attract. What does your audience survey tell you? Are there large geographical areas that you realise are under-presented in your analysis of attenders? Are there age brackets that you feel are missing, or groups – do you feel that school, adult or family groups have adequate representation? If you have social or community policies are you achieving them? Can you identify groups of people who you feel will help you achieve your aims?

7. Marketing

Marketing Resources: What is your budget? What staff are there to work on the marketing effort? Do you have any volunteers to help with any aspect of marketing? What equipment and resources do you have?

Marketing Approach: Stand back and take a cold critical look at your present marketing effort. Does your print do you justice? Is it saying enough about you? Is it taking the public's familiarity with you too much for granted? Is it old-fashioned - is it complacent?

What about your distribution – are you getting your print to as many places as possible, or could you do better? Are you spending too much, or enough on advertising – can you see any effect from that expenditure? Do your ads make the correct statement about you? Is your image appropriate for the sort of market you would like to see coming to your venue?

Marketing Activity: Outline your regular marketing activity. What do you do and when, and how often? Include: print; distribution; press activity; letters; mailing list; previews; use of other mailing lists; personal liaison work; talks; special events, etc. Anything you carry out which you feel contributes to informing the public about you.

When you have addressed all of these points and come up with answers in the form of statistics you have completed Part 1 of your marketing audit.

It is far simpler to conduct a marketing audit if there are research and intelligence systems in place or available to plug into. These can be very simple and inexpensive:

- Keeping a day-book enables staff to log; the weather, groups sizes, busiest periods, types of attenders, customers' comments, complaints, etc.

- Putting out simple survey forms can tell you about your visitors.

- Being on other gallery and museums mailing lists can keep you informed.

APPOINTING A MARKETING OFFICER

Members of the informal group of Marketing and Development Officers in Museums have commented in a survey upon the extremely elastic nature of their job descriptions, and the problems created by having a poor brief from management. For marketing officers with previous experience in the commercial sector, entering the world of museums can present something of a culture shock. Having a good job description is an important start for a new post. The description will probably need to be reviewed, even within six months of the start, because the problems and potential of the situation may only emerge once someone is actually doing the job.

Here are two job descriptions for new Marketing Officers' posts, and one Assistant Marketing Officer post. In both instances the jobs are evolving and the job descriptions being modified as they go along. Such changes should always be by agreement between officer and management. Look at the breadth of the first job – and note that it is part-time. This approach is not unusual, but it is optimistic.

JERSEY MUSEUMS SERVICE: PART-TIME MARKETING OFFICER

PURPOSE OF JOB – to develop and implement a marketing strategy for all the Jersey Museums Service sites; addressing the public perception of the Jersey Museums Service, its use by the whole community and maximising revenue within the constraints of the standards of quality, value, integrity and accessibility.

RESPONSIBLE TO   DIRECTOR

MAIN DUTIES:
> develop and implement an agreed corporate marketing strategy
> control the expenditure of the marketing budget
> devise and implement specific tactical campaigns
> devise and implement a programme of visitor research
> develop and promote trade relationships within the tourism industry
> identify and develop revenue opportunities within the corporate marketing strategy, specifically
> space hire
> business and private functions
> catering services
> shops
> co-ordinate and develop press and media relations in Jersey, the UK and Europe
> devise and develop promotional literature, organise and monitor distribution
> write advertising copy and press releases
> promote and organise community group visits
> co-ordinate an events programme to support the corporate marketing strategy
> assist with sponsorship developments

TYNE AND WEAR MUSEUMS: MARKETING OFFICER
GRADE	**SCALE 6/SO1**
RESPONSIBLE TO	**Principal Marketing & Commercial Officer**
RESPONSIBLE FOR	**Assistant Marketing Officer(s)**

GENERAL RESPONSIBILITY

To assist the Principal Marketing & Commercial Officer in the provision of a comprehensive, efficient and effective service for the marketing activities of Tyne and Wear Museums and in sponsorship and fundraising activities.

MAIN DUTIES

The following list is typical of the level of duties which the postholder will be expected to perform. It is not necessarily exhaustive and other duties of a similar type and level considered essential for the efficient and effective operation of the section may be required from time to time.

1 Make proposals for and seek approval of development of new markets, and increase responses and returns from existing markets within the overall policies and strategies adopted by Museums.

2 To propose and carry out research of appropriate markets.

3 To prepare written and statistical market analyses and plans.

4 Where necessary, to liaise with section colleagues, curators and other appropriate staff in the research and implementation of marketing activity.

5 To liaise closely with the Commercial Officer.

6 Under direction, and in liaison with Senior Curators, to assist in the co-ordination of initiatives in customer care.

7 Under direction, liaise with design staff in connection with the publishing activity of Tyne and Wear Museums.

8 Under direction, assist with the negotiation of publishing agreements with all appointed authors and publishing.

9 As required, and when necessary, utilising computer facilities, produce information showing market performance.

10 To assist in the preparation and up-dating of Business Plans for the section.

11 Under direction, seek out and maintain contact with external organisations who will seek or provide sponsorship for Tyne and Wear Museums' activities.

12 As required, and in conjunction with other sections/activities, organise fundraising activities and initiatives.

13 Establish and maintain appropriate financial documents and records in accordance with the financial and administrative requirements of Tyne and Wear Museums.

14 To compile and maintain mailing lists to serve the needs of all marketing operations.

15 To assist in the preparation of reports and prepare reports for the Principal Marketing and Commercial Officer as requested.

16 To maintain high standards of Health & Safety at Work and comply with relevant legislation.

TYNE AND WEAR MUSEUMS: ASSISTANT MARKETING OFFICER
GRADE   **SCALE 4/5**
RESPONSIBLE TO   **Marketing Officer**

GENERAL RESPONSIBILITY

To assist the Marketing Officer in the provision of a comprehensive, efficient and effective service for the marketing activities of Tyne and Wear Museums.

MAIN DUTIES

The following list is typical of the level of duties which the postholder will be expected to perform. It is not necessarily exhaustive and other duties of a similar type and level considered essential for the efficient and effective operation of the section may be required from time to time.

1 Contribute to the development of new markets, and increase responses and returns from existing markets within the overall policies and strategies adopted by Museums.

2 To carry out research of appropriate markets as requested.

3 To assist with the preparation of written and statistical market analyses and plans.

4 As directed and where necessary liaise with section colleagues, curators and other appropriate staff in the research and implementation of marketing activity.

5 As required assist with co ordination of initiatives in customer care.

6 As required assist with the compilation of marketing mailing lists.

7 To provide effective distribution of the Museums' promotional literature.

8 Assist in the staffing of outside functions aimed at promoting Museum events and exhibitions.

9 As required liaise with appointed advertising agencies and design studios.

10 To assist in the preparation and up-dating of Business Plans for the section.

11 The postholder will be expected to maintain high standards of Health & Safety at Work and comply with relevant legislation.

GLOSSARY OF COMMON MARKETING TERMS

(Reproduced from 'Marketing the Visual Arts' by permission of the Arts Council of Great Britain)

Consumers: People, the visitors and potential visitors to your gallery.

Consumer satisfaction: (customer satisfaction) When people respond positively to your product: ie enjoy visiting the gallery and feel they have experienced something of value.

Delivery mechanism: The means by which you reach people through your marketing; eg a leaflet, a special offer, or advertisement.

Direct marketing: A direct approach to a specific group of people (target market), usually by mail or telephone with a specially tailored marketing device such as a personalised letter.

Mail shot: A mailing of publicity material to a specific group of people (target market).

Marketing audit: An information gathering exercise to provide you with a clear description of your product, your target audiences, your competitor and your existing marketing resources.

Mission statement: A short description of your policy and objectives (what you want to do and who you want to do it for).

Performance indicators: Ways of measuring how far you have succeeded in what you set out to do; they might be numerical (visitor numbers) financial (bar sales) or to do with training etc.

Planning horizon: The time scale of how far ahead you can plan.

Product: What you are offering to your visitors. This includes not just an exhibition but also the building, the facilities, the staff: everything that makes up their experience of visiting.

Product proposition: How you express what you are offering: your message about your market.

Response mechanism: A device in a leaflet or piece of publicity that demands some kind of response from the reader (eg return a tear-off strip, make a phone-call), and allows you to quantify the level of response to your marketing tactic.

Target markets: The people you want to reach with your message: for marketing purposes they are normally divided into groups according to common features such as age, background, geographic location, etc.

ACORN CLASSIFICATIONS

(From the Acorn User Guide, published by CACI Information Services)

This system, unlike the more familiar ABC groupings according to the occupation of the head of the household, allows you to use the area or postcodes as a way to segment your market

Group A Agricultural Areas

These areas contain the 3% of the population who live in communities which depend directly on farming for their livelihood. They are usually situated too far from large towns to prove attractive to commuters.

Limited local job opportunities result in generally low household incomes and few chances for women to work. There are many cases of poor housing conditions and a large proportion of tenants live in tied cottages which lack basic amenities.

Low wages and the absence of retail competition result in somewhat unsophisticated consumer preferences and leisure is spent less through commercial outlets than in social activities and rural pursuits.

Although they are in the minority, the landowners in this group can, however, display a very wealthy profile.

Group B Modern Family Housing, Higher Incomes

The residents of these areas are primarily young families living in modern houses, very often on small private estates in commuter villages on the outskirts of large towns. The housing often suits the needs of people whose career advancement may require them to move to a different part of the country or who may expect to move to a larger house in a more select neighbourhood as their real incomes rise.

Incomes, car ownership and educational qualifications are all well above average in these areas and there is a tendency for people to travel considerable distance to work or shop. These factors, when combined with rapid population growth, result in relatively weak community networks and fairly high expenditure on consumer goods and family activities.

Group C Older Housing of Intermediate Status

This sort of area typically consists of older, mostly pre-1939 housing, which is not necessarily in poor condition, and contains a fairly representative cross-section of the population as a whole.

These areas often lie close to town centres with shops and local employment within easy reach, which compensates somewhat for the absence of large gardens and modern amenities. Generally the population is more elderly and less mobile than the national average and spends its time and money in more traditional ways than the younger families who have moved out to areas in Groups B and E.

Group D Older Terraced Housing

These areas are characterised by housing in pre-1914 terraced streets and tenements accommodating a high proportion of households living on very low incomes. Some of the housing still has no bath or inside WC and suffers from inadequate ventilation, heating and cooking facilities. Government grants and a migration of younger couples have more recently resulted in some modernisation, however. There is a lack of suitable areas where children can play.

In larger towns, these areas often house many young families who cannot afford or are unable to find other accommodation. In small towns, where traditional industries are often in decline, the areas contain a more settled, elderly population. There are few modern retail outlets here as such areas, characterised by declining population figures and low incomes, are not commercially attractive.

Group E Council Estates – Category I

The typical household in these areas consists of a young family with children often below school age, living in a modern, medium-sized house. This will have been built by the local authority of a new town development corporation. This type of area is most common on the outskirts of larger urban areas, to which companies and their skilled workforce have moved from congested inner areas during the past 30 years.

This movement away from relatives and the close community networks of the inner city often results in a weakening of traditional social attitudes, leisure patterns and consumer preferences. Thus the immediate family becomes a more important focus of leisure activity. Because of the higher wages and lower risk of unemployment, households become more confident in their ability to use credit to improve their living standards by purchasing consumer durables.

Group F Council Estates – Category II

These estates accommodate disproportionate numbers of manual, semi-skilled and unskilled workers and an above average concentration of disadvantaged groups such as the sick, handicapped, unemployed and single parents (if only because these groups are given preference in housing allocation policies).

Council estates in this group tend to house older couples and pensioners rather than young couples.

Although average incomes in these areas are low, in certain households disposable income will be higher as a result of there being several wage earners and low housing costs. Consumer preferences in these areas vary widely, but as a rule are more conservative than in Group E. Disposable income is higher than in Group G.

Group G   Council Estates – Category III

This Group comprises those council estates likely to have the most serious social problems, with exceptional levels of unemployment, overcrowding, large and single parent families and a widespread lack of private transport.

Such estates house large numbers of residents dependent upon the State for provision of such basic services.

Group H   Mixed Inner Metropolitan Areas

A high proportion of the country's ethnic minority population lives in this type of area, which comprises areas of typically pre-1914 housing, mostly in inner London. These areas suffer from a comparative shortage of adequate family accommodation with the result that low income households pay high rents for furnished flats or unfurnished terraced housing. Overcrowding is common, as is a lack of, and sharing of, basic amenities.

Though housing conditions are poor, employment opportunities are good with low unemployment, a high proportion of women at work and relatively high local wages in parts of inner London. A large number of residents are engaged in service trades, often in a self-employed capacity.

Group I   High Status Non-Family Areas

This type of area is found mostly in inner London and in university towns.

It comprises areas of older houses which have retained their high status; families have been replaced by single people and childless couples, often living in small flats in big old houses. Many of the people living here will be employed in varied and well-paid service jobs, located in the central business area.

Residents tend to be frequent readers of books and journals, receptive to new ideas and products. If they are single, they are likely to spend much of their leisure time and money on outside entertainment and on eating out.

Although incomes are well above average, they tend to be spent more frequently on luxury services than on consumer durables for which there is little space in a small flat.

Group J   Affluent Suburban Housing

In this housing Group, residents will tend to be older and on high incomes. The housing typically consists of suburban private housing, built between the wars, detached or semi-detached and well dispersed. These areas are most often found within the outer areas of large cities since a high proportion of workers are employed in professional or managerial jobs in the service sector.

As their children are often older or have even already left school (or university) and mortgages are low in relation to the value of the houses, the disposable income in such households is spent on luxury items and invested in home improvements and savings. Residents are attracted here by the peacefulness, privacy and exclusiveness of such areas.

Group K   Better-Off Retirement Areas

This Group includes those areas with a high proportion of elderly people. They may live in owner-occupied, detached or semi-detached houses, in seaside resorts or in blocks of private flats or sheltered accommodation elsewhere. A large proportion of these residents are of high social class and many have moved here on retiring.

Although the residents of such areas may be fairly wealthy, current expenditure is low, partly because households tend to be considerably smaller than the national average. A high proportion of expenditure is on specialist services, which therefore employ a disproportionate share of the active labour force.

INDEX

ACORN Classifications 138–41
Admission charges 24, 75–7
Advertising 17–24, 55
Advertising, design 22
Advertising, monitoring of 20, 54
Advertising, slot 20
Agency (advertising) role of 18
Art paper 53
Artwork 18, 51, 53

Bibliography 40–42
Binding 52
Budgets 24–7, 55

Canterbury Heritage Museum, case
 study 83–90
Checklist 8, 11–13, 26, 51, 62–3,
 72–3, 77–9
Classified advertising 18
'Cold calling' 30–31
Consultancy, short-term case
 studies 83–90, 101–10
Consultants, role of 15, 70–72
Competitiveness 75
Copywriting 52, 73–4
Corporate identity 27–30, 55
Creativity 14–15, 74–5
Customer care (quality of service)
 57, 72, 124–7

Discounts 37–38, 42, 44
Display advertising 18
Distribution 30–32, 55
Dummy 52

Emergency plans 32–6, 55
Evaluation 54–7

Focus groups 49
Flyposting 32
Fundraising 36–7, 55

Glossary 137
Group travel 37–9, 55

Half-tone 52
Housestyle 28

Incentives 42–4

Job descriptions, marketing officers
 131–5
Joint schemes 44–5, 55, 91–100

Lobbying (opinion-informing) 37,
 57, 59–61
Logos 27–30

Mailing lists 31–2
Manchester Museum of Science &
 Industry, policy 111–19, 124–7
Marketing brief 10–12
'Marketing led' 7
Marketing officer, appointments
 131–4
Marketing plans, examples
 111–19, 119–23
Market research 45–9, 65, 68
Marketing strategy, how to write
 7–15, 67, 129–31
Monitoring 54–7
Museums Alive!, case study
 91–100

National Code of Practice for
 Visitor Attractions 72
New markets 57–9

Offset Litho 53

Pantone colours 53
Paper sizes 52

PMT   53
Positioning (designing the strategy)   11
Press relations   32–6, 61–4, 65
Pricing (yield)   75–7
Printed material (literature)   49–54, 56

Quotability (sound bites)   65

Readership   20
Reading capability   73
Regiments of Gloucester Museum, marketing plan   119–23
Reversed out (printing)   53

Ruddington Village Museum, case study   101–10

Situational analysis   8, 11
Surveys   8, 45
SWOT analysis   8–10, 12, 13

Targeting   14, 42, 58, 68–70, 138–141
Tourist Information Centres   30, 50

Value for money   72

Yorkshire & Humberside Museums, case study   91–100

Printed in the United Kingdom for HMSO
Dd295266 4/94 C21 G531 10170